The Sun in Astrology

The Ultimate Guide to the Giver of Life, Its Role in Vedic Astrology, and Sun Sign

Your Free Gift (only available for a limited time)

Thanks for getting this book! If you want to learn more about various spirituality topics, then join Mari Silva's community and get a free guided meditation MP3 for awakening your third eye. This guided meditation mp3 is designed to open and strengthen ones third eye so you can experience a higher state of consciousness. Simply visit the link below the image to get started.

https://spiritualityspot.com/meditation

Contents

Introduction

The brightest star we can observe, the Sun, is a stationary celestial body that governs the planets in our solar system. Despite being cold and hot, the Sun gives life to humans, and survival without it is simply impossible. This massive illuminating source of life is a projection of humans to the outer world. It is every soul's identity and a navigating channel that helps one find the right direction. While it remains stationary and governs other bodies that orbit around it, the Sun also propels influential energy to help us become more confident and build the courage to fight adversities. This energy is one of the many reasons why the Sun is significant in the realm of astrology.

All bodies and energies revolve around the Sun. Whereas the Sun represents masculine energy, the Moon portrays a feminine role. The Sun's energy influences all the male figures in a family (father, son, husband, and brother). The ruler of the solar system also represents higher power, royalty, and vitality. It influences people to maintain their health and stay mentally and spiritually fit.

The importance of the Sun and its energy has been glorified for centuries. While some worshipped the Sun for its mighty demeanor, others held it as a subject of interest and curiosity. Ancient scholars and analytical learners even studied this celestial body's path of motion to draw birth charts and determine a person's fate and characteristics upon birth. What's more, the Sun's position and movement have also been codified to devise a calendrical system based on solar cycles to tell time. The first calendar was designed centuries ago, tracing the path of solar and lunar cycles to calculate time and accurately determine hours, days, weeks, and years. The Gregorian calendar, the modern calendar we all use, is inspired by ancient solar calendars.

Many scholars even drew parallels between the Sun's energy and humans' health, which was also the diverging point of Vedic astrology. It was believed that the Sun's affliction could help doctors diagnose physical health problems, most of which were related to the heart. Over time, the body's energy manifested into the life of humans by amalgamating it with yoga. For centuries, Surya Namaskars have been some of the most effective yoga practices to help treat a person's mental and spiritual health. The poses and asanas were directly linked to the body's chakras, which helped the healing process.

Today, the Sun is still perceived as one's identity. People consider reading their sun signs and determining their characteristics or fate to predict their near future. The Sun represents Leo due to its fiery and strong nature, but it also has strong connections with several other zodiac signs. By tapping into the Sun's energy, you can revitalize your mind and body and become more self-aware. If you can successfully achieve this, it means you have to be blessed with a creative, fulfilling, and conscious mind.

We've only scratched the surface of some of these interesting topics about the Sun and its astrological significance. These will be elaborated on further throughout this book. Every chapter is categorized based on the Sun's distinct roles in astrology and as the giver of life. In this book, you will learn about the Sun as seen by different cultures and during different periods, branches of astrology, and its significance in various civilizations. You will also discover how the Sun has been used as a timekeeping tool since time immemorial, its relationship with zodiac signs, as well as effective ways to harness its energy and manifest the positive changes in your life.

Read on to explore the significance of the Sun in astrology and its role in all other aspects of our lives.

Chapter 1: Sun as the Giver of Life

Apart from being an astronomical body that provides us with the light and warmth necessary to sustain all life on Earth, the Sun has also played a major role in how human religion and spirituality have evolved over the centuries. Nearly all major ancient religions worshipped the Sun or a solar deity associated with the Sun.

These deities were often marked as uniquely powerful, and – like the Egyptian solar deity, Ra – were usually either the head of their pantheon or considered main leaders in it. Some ancient belief systems took the concept of solar deities one step further into actual sun worship, including the short-lived Atomism that dominated ancient Egypt in the 14th century B.C.

The Importance of the Sun in Ancient Civilizations

Just as the Moon is considered an aspect of the sacred feminine element in many ancient religions, the Sun is considered the sacred masculine element. The Sun was essential to the ancient way of life, and many civilizations deemed it the most powerful element in the world so that their lives were designed to make as much use of the Sun's energies as possible.

The ancient Egyptians designed their homes to store the Sun's heat in the walls so that their homes would stay warm at night. The sun's heat was especially crucial, seeing as desert nights can become very cool, very fast.

The Greeks, Romans, Native Americans, and ancient Chinese used similar techniques when building their homes. In fact, Socrates taught classes on building and architecture to make the best use of the Sun's life-giving heat. The Greeks built buildings with windows facing south to ensure they got the most of the Sun's heat and insulated their north walls (which received the least heat).

The Romans used similar techniques when building their baths, with many baths featuring southern walls made entirely of windows to ensure they got the most solar energy possible. The Anasazi used their knowledge of how the Sun worked to provide their homes with heat during winters and shade in the summer. The homes in Mesa Verde show just how well Native Americans leveraged solar principles to build communities.

Prehistoric Chinese homes would often only open to the south of the structure. This positioning kept the cold north winds out and allowed them to take advantage of as much of the Sun's heat as possible.

Ultimately, the Sun's importance was undeniably linked to its ability to generate, nurture, and sustain life across time and cultures. It was so important that cultures built structures to track its movements, including the pyramids, standing stones, and other earthworks. It's no surprise that these structures are also often seen as spiritually important. After all, the Sun's nourishment of life also included nourishment of the spiritual and mental aspects of life.

The Spiritual Importance of the Sun across Civilizations

As mentioned, the Sun was often the masculine counterpart to the Moon. Most solar deities were male, which reinforced their importance in the ancient world.

The Sun is the planetary force that bestows life and light upon the Earth; it was often regarded as all-seeing. It was linked to justice, enlightenment, illumination, and wisdom. Apollo, the best-known of the Greek solar deities, was also the god of prophecy, the truth, and divine justice.

Given these traits – justice, knowledge, power, and wisdom – the Sun and sun gods were often associated with divine kingship. Countless kings and rulers claimed to be direct descendants of the Sun, which helped them consolidate and ensure their power, and many solar deities were associated with the Supreme Deity of a given pantheon.

For example, in Egyptian mythology, Ra is the dominant of all the gods. He is the king of gods and is considered the creator and nourisher of the Earth. Similarly, in India, the sun god Surya was an all-seeing god who expelled darkness and disease from the world.

In later Roman history, solar worship took prominence, and nearly all deities worshipped during the period (including ones as distinct as Mithras and Christ) were ascribed solar qualities. The Romans celebrated the feast of Sol Invictus (the "Unconquered Sun") each year on December 25th, and this festival would later be co-opted as Christmas.

In the Americas, solar deities were just as prominent. The Plains Indians of North America celebrated the Sun Dance, one of their most important religious ceremonies, while pre-Columbian civilizations in Mexico and Peru involved sun worship, with the Sun playing an important role in both religions and rituals. Peruvian rulers were considered to be incarnations of Inti, the God of the Sun.

While the Aztecs practiced human sacrifice in honor of the sun deities Huitzilopochtli and Tezcatlipoca, the Japanese sun goddess Amaterasu was considered one of the leaders of the Japanese pantheon. She was also the tutelary deity of the Japanese imperial family, and the Japanese state uses solar symbolism as part of its national symbolism until this day.

As demonstrated by Amaterasu, not all solar deities and Sun gods were male. The Sun was a nourisher and giver of life, similar to the role women played and continue to play among humans. Because of this, several female solar deities, including female deities who were not necessarily Sun goddesses but were closely linked to the solar deities of their pantheon.

For instance, in ancient Egyptian religion, the sun disk (a symbol of the Sun) was carried not only by the solar deity Ra but also by numerous female deities associated with him, including:

- **Sekhmet,** the lion-headed daughter of Ra
- **Wadjet,** one of the patron goddesses to the king and the tutelary goddess of Lower Egypt
- **Hathor/Hesat,** the sky goddess who was one of the Eyes of Ra, and acted as either Ra's consort or mother
- **Isis,** one of the best-known Egyptian goddesses, was considered the divine mother of the pharaoh (the Egyptian pharaoh was linked to Horus, Isis's divine son with her consort Osiris). She was also the goddess of magic and wisdom, which were abilities she received in return for curing Ra of snake venom, and both of which are traditionally linked to solar deities.

Sekhmet

Other ancient religions that boast female solar deities include several Native American tribes, including the Cherokee (who worship Unelanuhi), Inuit (who venerate Malina), and Miwok (whose solar deity is Heklooas).

The solar deity in Germanic mythology is often female, while the Moon deity is male. In Old High German myth, the solar deity is the goddess Sunna, while the goddess Sól (also named Sunna and Frau Sonne) is the deity who pulls the Sun through the sky on her chariot. Likewise, the Aboriginal people of Australia generally regard the Sun as female, with solar deities including Bila, worshipped by the Adnyamathanha.

Solar Deities across Civilizations

While solar deities shared common characteristics, their treatment, mythologies, and worship differed across cultures. Some of the best-known solar deities include:

Helios and Apollo in Greek Mythology

Greek mythology featured two prominent solar deities: Helios and Apollo. Of the two, Helios was the older and was considered the personification of the Sun, rather than just a deity who ruled it; same case with Apollo.

While Apollo was a son of Zeus, Helios was a deity from the generation before the gods and was one of the Titans. Helios was the son of the Titans Hyperion and Theia. He was -technically - cousin to the eldest gods (Zeus, Hera, Poseidon, Demeter, Hades, and Hestia), as well as brother to Selene and Eos, the personifications of the Moon and the Dawn.

Helios

While Helios and his siblings were relatively minor gods in Classical Greece, his worship became more prominent toward late antiquity. He was made the central deity of Roman Emperor Julian's religious cult in the 4th century A.D.

However, it should be noted that despite his relatively minor status, the ancient Greeks were still well aware of the importance he held as a solar deity. He features numerous mythological tales, including ones as well known as the abduction of Persephone and the story of Heracles.

Helios was often linked to other Greek deities, including Apollo and Zeus, the king of the gods. Some authors, including Hesiod, directly reference Helios as being "Zeus's eye," while an Orphic saying links Zeus, Hades, and Helios (in his form as Helios-Dionysus) with joint sovereignty. He was also linked to Cronus, father of the eldest gods and known as Saturn in ancient Rome.

Another prominent reference to Helios comes in the form of the Greek Magical Papyri. These are a collection of magic spells, hymns, and rituals used between the 2nd century BC and the 5th century AD. In them, Helios is considered the source and creator of life. He is given far broader powers than in traditional Greek myth and is revered as the lord of the heavens and the cosmos and the god of the sea.

In this collection of papyri, Helios was also said to take the form of 12 hours, each representing an hour of the day. This representation links him directly to the zodiac. He is also sometimes assimilated with the Roman god Mithras and is combined into Helios-Mithras. In this role, he is said to have revealed the secrets of immortality to the author of the text. He is also often linked with the Egyptian god Ra due to his journey on a sun boat and his actions in "restraining the serpent" (usually linked to Ra's eternal battle against Apep/Apophis).

Other links in the papyri include one to the Hebrew god Yahweh. He is the Agathodaimon, "the god of gods," linked to the Egyptian Horus in his role as Horus Harpocrates. Helios is often referred to as Iao, a name derived from Yahweh, and shares many of his epithets.

Apollo, on the other hand, is a different deity altogether. One tale that explains his link to the Sun despite the existence of Helios in the Greek pantheon comes through the tale of Phaeton, one of the sons of Helios.

When Helios allowed his son to drive his solar chariot, he could not control the vehicle, resulting in the devastation of the Earth. In response, Zeus killed the boy with a lightning bolt to save humanity and other life on Earth. In his grief, Helios refused to take up his duties as the driver of the sun chariot, leaving Apollo to replace him in this role.

Apollo is a manifold god with authority over domains such as archery, poetry, music and dance, healing, and disease. He is also the deity of the Sun and the light, and he holds dominion over prophecy, the truth, and the revelation of mysteries.

In his role as the sun god, Apollo was endowed with numerous designations. These include Phobos ("bright), Helius ("sun"), Aegletes ("light of the sun"), Lyceus ("light," an epithet also associated with Leto, mother of Apollo and his twin Artemis), Sol ("sun" in Latin), and Phanaeus ("giving or bringing light"). As the god of prophecy, he was also referred to as Coelispex (a combination of the Latin words for "sky" and "to look at").

Apollo's worship was not limited to the ancient Greeks, though. He was one of the few gods that remained relatively similar for the Romans, keeping both his name and his function (the other deity to do so was Gaia/Gaea, the personification of the Earth and one of the Greek primordial deities).

Following the growth and expansion of the Roman Empire, Apollo's worship spread across the Roman kingdom and was particularly prominent among the Celts. Like with the Greeks and Romans, he was primarily seen as a sun god and a god of healing. His epithets by the Celts include Apollo Atepomarus ("the great horseman" - in the Celtic world, horses were linked to the Sun), Apollo Belenus "bright, brilliant," a manifestation of his role as god of healing and of the Sun), Apollo Grannus (a spring god of healing), and Apollo Virotutis ("benefactor of mankind").

Apollo was one of the few gods to have multiple cult sites, his first being at Delos (his birthplace in myth) and Delphi (where he slew the monster Python, and home to Pythia, also known as the Oracle of Delphi.

Delphi, this oracle, was the major Greek oracle referenced multiple times in Greek myth). There were also multiple well-known temples in honor of Apollo throughout the Greek and Roman worlds, including ones at:

- Thebes
- Eretria
- Thermon
- Syracuse (Sicily)
- Delphi
- Hamaxitus
- Apollonia Pontica
- Pompeii
- Rome

Shamash in Mesopotamian Mythology

Also known as Utu, Shamash was an ancient Mesopotamian sun god. He was also the god of justice, morality, and truth. Along with his father Sin (God of the Moon) and his twin sister Inanna (also known as Ishtar, the Goddess of the planet Venus, love, beauty, and power, and the Queen of Heaven), he formed an astral triad of deities.

Shamash

As a solar deity, Shamash had dominion over justice and equity. He was revered as the bringer of light, defeater of darkness and evil, and was given the right to judge both gods and men. One legend holds that it was Shamash who gave the Babylonian king Hammurabi his famous code of laws.

Shamash was also considered a bestower of life and light. He was the governor of the entire universe and was one of the only purely heroic figures in Mesopotamian mythology. Due to this, he rarely figured in mythological tales, which instead focused on how gods behave similarly to mortals.

The oldest documents mentioning Shamash (in his role as Utu) were traced back to 3500 BC and also represented some of the first known written Mesopotamian scriptures. He was worshipped for over 3000 years until the fall of Mesopotamian culture.

His main temples were located in Sippar and Larsa, and he was known to be a kind, generous deity. He was considered one of the protectors of the kings of Uruk and played a role in helping Gilgamesh defeat the ogre Huwawa (also known as Humbaba) in the

Epic of Gilgamesh. His consort was Aya, who would later be absorbed into the figure of his twin sister, Inanna/Ishtar.

Surya and Savitr in Hindu Mythology

In Hindu mythology, Surya is the chief solar deity and is also known by the names Aditya, Visvasat ("brilliant"), Mitra, and Savitr ("nourisher," though Savitr is also identified as a distinct deity in scriptures such as the Rig Veda).

Surya is first mentioned in one of the oldest surviving Vedic hymns in the Rig Veda, where he is worshipped as the rising Sun and is considered a dispeller of darkness, the deity of all life and one who brings knowledge.

Surya

In the Vedic texts, Surya is the creator of Prakriti or the material universe. He is often part of a trinity of deities, alongside Agni (god of fire) and either Vayu (god of wind) or Indra (god of lightning, thunder, and rains, and the king of the gods). Together, these three deities from the Brahman, a metaphysical concept that symbolizes the eternal truth and the Ultimate Reality in Hindu philosophy.

The figure of Surya was originally several other solar deities, which fused into a single figure. Hence deities like Savitr, Mitra, Aditya, and Pushan are occasionally seen as distinct deities from Surya.

He is also an important figure in Indian astronomy and astrology. In astrology, he is part of the Navagraha, a Hindu zodiac system. He has been one of the primary deities in Hinduism for a significant part of the religion's history. The worship of Surya only declined in the 13th century, likely due to the Muslim conquest of and influence over northern India. He would be replaced in importance by deities like Vishnu and Shiva.

However, numerous Surya temples have survived in the Indian subcontinent, especially in South India. He is still an important deity in this part of the country and remains important to Tamils, who worship him during the harvest festival of Pongal. Other major celebrations linked to Surya include Makar Sankranti, Kumbh Mela, and Chhath Puja.

As mentioned, Savitr is sometimes identified as distinct from Surya, especially in older texts like the Rig Veda. He is symbolic of the Sun before sunrise, while Surya symbolizes the Sun after it has risen. He also represents the life-giving power of the Sun, which is perhaps a reason behind his veneration.

The Rig Veda dedicates 11 hymns to Savitr, and his name is mentioned about 170 times in the text. Of the 11 hymns, Hymn 35 is perhaps the most detailed in its adoration of Savitr and is also known as the "Hymn of Savitr."

Additionally, Savitr is celebrated in the Gayatri Mantra. This hymn is one of the most sacred and best-known in Hinduism and is also among the most powerful. One of the many translations of the hymn into English comes from the Indologist Ralph T.H. Griffith, who translates it as: "*May we attain that excellent glory of Savitr the god: So may He stimulate our prayers.*"

It should be noted that while Savitr stopped being considered an independent deity by the end of the Vedic period and was instead completely subsumed by Surya, he is still worshipped due to these hymns.

In some traditions of modern Hinduism, Savitr is worshipped as Savitri, and the Gayatri Mantra is also known as the Savitri Mantra. In these traditions, this deity is female rather than male, and the understanding of the hymn changes accordingly. Another translation of the hymn comes from the Indian monk and nationalist figure, Swami Vivekananda, who translated it as: "*We meditate on the glory of that Being who has produced this universe; may She enlighten our minds.*"

Lastly, in modern Vedic astrology, the Sun is considered a representative of the soul. Just as solar deities were considered bringers of light, the Sun is the bringer of an inner "solar light" and represents leadership, self-confidence, power, and health in Vedic astrology. Charts that include the Sun in an advantageous position can often indicate that the chart's owner possesses clarity about spiritual matters.

Chapter 2: The Sun as the Timekeeper

As one of the most significant celestial bodies in astronomy and astrology, ancient scholars and locals used the Sun star to tell the time. With the absence of a reliable way to tell the time and carry out daily activities like sleeping, eating, growing crops, and figuring out the seasons, people followed the Sun's path to determine specific points during the day or night. As they realized the importance of marking a solar and lunar cycle to ascertain the day, week, and year, ancient scholars dug deeper and designed their own calendars with specific days and hours to achieve a better sense of time. This innovation allowed commoners to harvest crops based on specific seasons, migrate, and carry out other important activities.

The Concept of Time Based on the Sun's Movement

Many ancient civilizations drafted certain methods to tell time. While some designed tools and devices to locate the Sun's movement, others simply told the time by looking at the placement of other stars and using their instincts.

The Position of the Sun and Stars

Ancient astrologers told the time by locating the position of the Moon, stars, the Sun, and the five planets in the sky. A lunar cycle comprises different phases of the Moon and covers around 30 days of a month. Similarly, the sun's position was determined to denote the "solstice," when the Sun is at the farthest distance and rises or sets across the horizon. At one point, both the sunrise and sunset take place at the closest point, which produces a reverse effect. Over a specific period, this pattern can be traced to form rough circles on the ground and determine the month or year, which is exactly what our ancestors did.

In parallel, some visible stars and constellations were also studied to note the location of the Sun and the Moon. Ancient engineers and architects used this astrological information to design buildings according to the celestial bodies' position and movement. These periods were also considered auspicious or holy, marking when our ancestors carried out important tasks like migrating, trading, and harvesting. The Antikythera mechanism is a device made of wheels and gears believed to be used by ancient scholars to measure eclipses and the Sun's exact position.

Sundial

The first sundials can be dated back to 1500 BC when ancient scholars had designed a tool to tell the time based on the Sun's movement and position. It is known that ancient Egyptians were among the first to craft a sundial to tell the time. Even though the identity of the pioneers is undefined, accounts claim that the Jews, Babylonians, or the Egyptians were the first to use (if not design) this exemplary tool. While the Jews and the Babylonians used a 7-day week system to tell the time, the Romans came up with eight days; the last day is dedicated to buying and selling possessions.

Over time, the Greeks and Romans redesigned the sundial to produce more accurate results. While ancient designs only showed the months of a year, newer modifications divided the sections into specific hours and units. Typically, ancient sundials were designed in four shapes - conical, hemispherical, planar, and cylindrical. The sundial's surface divided the sections into different angles and latitudes, representing specific quadrants or quarters of an hour. Basically, the Sun's shadow on the sundial was the prime time-telling factor. Over time, portable and public sundials also became popular.

Water Clocks

Since sundials could not tell the time during cloudy days or at night, ancient Romans came up with another way to tell the time even when the Sun was not visible. They drew inspiration from sundials and made a water clock with similar calibrations. This device, called the "clepsydra," measured time based on the flow of liquid collected by a vessel. Using this, the outflow and inflow of the liquid were measured to indicate the passage of time based on the bowl's markings. As the water level rose in the bowls, the observer could tell the time thanks to the lines. This design was used in the 5th century with modern pieces using pendulums.

Water clocks gained popularity worldwide through trade, and every region developed its own version of the revolutionary time-telling device. Regions like Persia, India, China, Babylon, and Egypt developed distinct design features that helped the locals tell the time without waiting for the sun to shine. These design elements were further modified over time to get more precise results. For centuries, water clocks remained the most reliable and accurate way of telling time, which is why they were used for over a millennium.

The Development of Calendar Systems around the World

Various calendar systems around the world were developed based on the Sun's position and movement. The solar calendar typically relies on the time it takes the Earth to complete one full rotation around the Sun, which is 365 ¼ days or one year.

Babylonian and Persian Calendars

The Persians have always been curious about the Sun's movement, which led to the design of their calendar using a solar approach. Unlike other cultures that also emphasized the importance of lunisolar and lunar cycles, the Persians and Babylonians only focused on the solar cycle. This focus partly stems from the significance of the folklore "Cyrus the Great" and the holy symbol of the Sun in ancient Persian culture. Ancient Persians devised a calendar based on the movement and observation of the Sun, where one year spanned 360 days. The months were divided based on a lunar cycle, with two to three sections over 30 days.

While no official names were given to the days, every month was designated with the name of a significant festival. To align the seasons with the calendrical system, the Persians added an extra month every six years. Between 650 and 330 BC (the late Achaemenid period), the Empire needed a practical timekeeping system based on ancient Egyptian belief. The most significant days of every month were set aside for the worship of Ahura Mazda, the supreme god of the Zoroastrian religion.

The Egyptian Calendar

Among all cultures and civilizations, the Egyptians were one of the first to devise a calendar based on the Sun's movements and position. According to the Egyptian calendar, one year comprised 365 days, divided into three parts or seasons. Every season spanned approximately 120 days along with an intercalary month. One month comprised 30 days, and four of these months made one season. Collectively, the year was made up of 12 months, which were named after the significant festivals of that time. One month was divided into three "decans," each decan comprising ten days. In the past, royal artisans and merchants enjoyed the last two days of every decan to be off-duty and relax, which is perceived as the modern form of the weekend.

Initially, ancient Egyptians divided one year into 13 months based on the solar cycle. Like the modern calendar, the Egyptian calendrical system had 365 days as one year, unlike the Gregorian system, where one year was 365 ¼ days. This system resulted in the loss of one entire day every four years. Over time, the concept of "Leap Day" was introduced, where an extra day was added to the fourth year to compensate for the loss. However, climatic and natural observations made by experts led to the modern version of the calendar system that is considered the most accurate calendar of all.

The Greek Calendar

Ancient Greek scholars devised different calendar systems based on the understandings and ideals of every region. Among all these, the Athenian calendar is the most popular design to date. The Athenians devised their calendar based on the position of the Moon and the Sun, known as the lunisolar year system. Every 12 lunar cycles in order were regarded as one year, with the No Moon and Full Moon being the start and end of each phase, respectively. Depending on a cycle's duration, one month was considered as either 29 days or 30 days alternately.

In the beginning, the Athenian calendar only had 12 months. Over time, it added a 13th month to the year. The 13 months in order were called Hekatombaion, Metageitnion, Boedromion, Pyanepsion, Maimakterion, Poseidon I, Poseidon II, Gamelion, Anthesterion, Elaphebolion, Munychion, Thargelion, and Skirophorion. Instead of dividing the entire month into weeks, Greeks divided the period of 29/30 days into three parts, with each part comprising ten days. Every month started with a day named "Noumenia" and ended with a day called "the old and the new." Since the Lunar year and Solar year encompassed 354 days, 8 hours, and 365 days, 5 hours, and 48 minutes, respectively, ancient Greek scholars could not align the calendars based on both systems. To solve this problem, they introduced the 13th month, coined the "embolismic month." Although the calendar was not accurate, it was followed for a long time until specific changes were introduced, and the locals began using the Roman calendar for timekeeping.

The Roman Calendar

The ancient Roman calendar stemmed from the Greek timetable with some modifications rooted in Roman beliefs and learnings. Their calendar was first introduced in the 8th century BCE by Rome's first ruler, Romulus. One year was spread across a period of 304 days and ignored the mid-winter period of 61 days. The 304 days were divided into ten months: Martius, Aprilis, Maius, Junius, Quintilis, Sextilis, September, October, November, and December. Over time, as Numa Pompilius took over Rome, he added the missing 61 days and divided them into two months, called January and February.

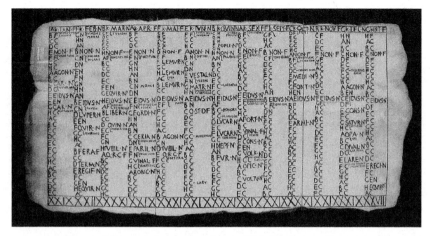

According to Numa, the calendar still failed to adhere to the solar year, which is why he forced the addition of Mercedonus, an extra month in every year. It was added after the 23rd or 24th day of February, thereby pushing the last days of the month even further. In turn, every year ended up having 22 to 23 additional days, which aligned with the concept of a solar year. The Romans were so proud of the timekeeping design that they adorned it on walls and carved its tabular form in stone. The Kalends, the Nones, and the Ides were the three main points of a month, and the days were denoted by names or letters.

The Assyrian Calendar

Compared to other cultures and their calendars, the Assyrian calendar was quite ahead of its time and partly inspired by the Babylonian calendar. It was first recognized in the 1950s, with 4750 BC being the fixed era due to the prominence of the Middle Ubaid period, during which the locals built the first temple at their sacred place, Ashur. Unlike other calendars that mark the beginning of a year around the winter season, the Assyrian calendar starts in the spring. The locals still gather during their New Year's Day and celebrate with food and significant rituals. December 2019 was marked as the Assyrian calendar's 6769th year.

Essentially, if you want to calculate the current Assyrian year, add the number 4750 to the current Gregorian year. This system was used in other parts of the Middle East, such as modern-day Syria, Iraq, Palestine, Lebanon, and Jordan. Every month in this calendar is represented in order by the Month of Happiness, Love, Building, Harvesting, Ripening of Fruits, Sprinkling of Seeds, Giving, Awakening of Buried Seeds, Conceiving, Resting, Flooding, and Evil Spirits. While some months cover 30 days, others can span 29 or 31 days.

Some of these calendar systems vanished with time, yet others were modified and redesigned with modern findings and calculations to devise a precise timekeeping schedule. As you can see, almost every calendar system was designed with similar calculations and holds specks of the modern timekeeping pattern. The calendar we use today was influenced by the past, encompassing many significant learnings based on the movements of the Sun and the Moon.

The Panchanga - Five Limbs of Time

The Panchanga (or the Five Limbs of Time) used in Vedic astrology are significant to Hindu mythology and various cultures. Some astrologers still use the Panchanga system to devise astrological birth charts and determine a person's fate upon birth. The Five Limbs of Time are Tithi (Date), Karan (Half of Tithi), Vaar (Day), Yoga, and Nakshatra (Constellation). Each limb is determined based on every planet's location, movement, and interaction with the Sun and the Moon. Nowadays, astrologers create a tabulated version of each limb to formulate the Panchang and apply it to determine the best days to conduct auspicious celebrations.

Tithi - Date

Every Lunar day in a Hindu calendar is denoted as Tithi. To calculate a Tithi, astrologers observe the Moon's position and alignment with the Sun. When it moves up to 12 degrees to the east, a Tithi is devised. The 15 Tithis in a month are named Pratipada,

Dwitiya, Tritiya, Chaturthi, Panchami, Shasthi, Saptami, Ashtami, Navami, Dasami, Ekadasi, Dwadasi, Trayodasi, Chaturdasi, Purnima, and Amavasya (in order). The New Moon or No Moon Day is called Amavasya, which occurs when the Sun and the Moon's longitudes align. These Tithis represent one day each within a fortnight, covering 15 days in a month.

The first Tithi occurs during the Moon's waxing phase and is referred to as the Pratipada Thithi. As the Moon shifts away from the Sun, it positions itself at a 180-degree linear point, marking the Full Moon or Purnima. The length of every Tithi varies due to the Moon and Sun's changing speeds and locations. While some Tithis are calculated as less than 22 hours, others can stretch up to 26 hours.

Karan

The half of a Tithi, a Karan, is calculated when the Moon moves up to 6 degrees from the Sun. It is divided into two categories, Sthira (fixed) and Charan (movable). With this, one month comprises 30 Tithis and 60 Karans. The first seven movable Karans are called Bava, Balava, Kaulava, Taitula, Garija, Vanija, and Visti, and the four fixed Karans are named Sakuna, Chatushpada, Naga, and Kimstughna. As the month passes, each Karan occurs in order and ends with a Tithi.

A person born under a specific Karan will display distinct characteristics throughout their life. Like a Tithi is determined to proceed with an auspicious ceremony, a Karan is also calculated to find the right "Muhurta" or time. While people use Tithis to determine a favorable hour or day, a Karan can help decipher a person's personality. The movable Karans occur almost eight times in a lunar cycle or one month. On the other hand, fixed Karans are constant and are generally considered inauspicious.

Vaar - Day

One Vaar or day is calculated as 24 hours, totaling seven Vaars in a week. Every hour is one Hora. As the sun rises, a Vaar starts and ends with another sunrise. The seven Vaars are named after the ruling planet of each day, namely Sunday, Monday, Tuesday, Wednesday, Thursday, Friday, and Saturday, named after Sun, Mercury (or the Moon in some cases), Venus, Earth, Mars, Jupiter, and Saturn, respectively. In the Hindu calendar, the Vaars are called Ravivaar, Somvaar, Mangalvaar, Budhvaar, Guruvaar, Shukravaar, and Shanivaar.

Since the Sun is located at the center and governs all other planets, the first Vaar of a week starts with Sunday or Ravivaar. This system shows why the first Hora is significant to the Sun. While the Moon, Venus, Jupiter, and Mercury project a mild and kind temperament to their respective Vaars, the Sun, Saturn, and Mars can be harsh and cruel. The former planets allow you to execute auspicious activities, whereas the other planets provide strength and the opportunity to accomplish difficult feats. The 7 Vaars are universal and are used to delimit today's working calendar.

Nakshatra - Constellation

Nakshatras are Lunar constellations that cover the sky's 360-degree spread. With each constellation covering 13.20 degrees, the entire sky totals 27 Nakshatras. In specific order, they are called Ashwini, Bharani, Krittika, Rohini, Mrigasira, Aarudra, Punarvasu, Pushya, Aslesha, Magha, Purva Phalguni, Uttara Phalguni, Hasta, Chitra, Swati, Vishakha, Anuradha, Jyestha, Moola, Poorvashada, Uttarashada, Sravana, Dhanishta, Satabisha, Poorva Bhadrapada, Uttara Bhadrapada, and Revati. Every Nakshatra is housed in four quarters or Padas, which collectively cover 20 minutes and 3 degrees.

Every constellation represents a particular deity, gemstone, color, and Lord or planet. Astrologers study the Padas, Rashis, and Nakshatras to determine the most favorable times for conducting celebrations, moving to a new house, getting married, or starting a business.

Yoga

When the Sun and the Moon separate, their distance is measured over specific periods to determine the Yoga. Formally known as Nithya Yoga, this limb is calculated by adding the Sun and Moon's longitude and dividing it by 13.20. The 27 Yogas identified in Vedic astrology are Vishkambha, Preeti, Ayushman, Saubhagya, Shobhana, Atiganda, Sukarma, Dhriti, Shoola, Ganda, Vriddhi, Dhruva, Vyaghata, Harshana, Vajra, Siddhi, Vyatipata, Variyana, Parigha, Shiva, Siddha, Sadhya, Shubha, Shukla, Brahma, Indra, and Vaidhriti.

Nine of the Yogas are deemed inauspicious, which is when people refrain from celebrations or acquiring new possessions. Among the 18 remaining Yogas, each entity represents a different aspect of life. While some symbolize health and happiness, others stand for growth, success, and splendor. In some versions of Vedic astrology, the Yogas are defined according to the rising and setting time of the Sun, which can affect a person's fate and bring changes to their personality when they are born.

The Five Limbs are not just significant to a person's birth. They also mark auspicious dates for starting a new business, getting married, or harvesting crops during peak season. Some astrologers devise the Panchang so that the person can also be wary of the inauspicious hours or days to avoid any celebration. These include Lagna Pravesh charts, Varjyam, Durmuhurtham, and Rahukalam, which are based on the movement of specific planets and their locations within the active houses.

Chapter 3: Vedic Astrology and the Sun

In Hindu and Vedic astrology, the Sun is the source of livelihood and the main energy of the cosmos. Since it is the essence of living, it is considered the most powerful body of all, especially in Hindu mythology and Vedic astrology. Since Vedic astrologers still devise natal charts based on the Sun's movement, many people hold this unique celestial body in high regard.

The Sun in the Exaltation and Debilitation State According to Vedic Astrology

The position of the Sun in a horoscope varies from person to person, determined by the time of their birth. While some charts display an exalted Sun, others portray a debilitated planet. An exalted Sun is the strongest and exudes a powerful personality. The Sun sits in every zodiac sign for one month. It takes one year for the Sun to complete a full zodiac cycle and transit from one sign to another in different directions. For example, it moves in the northern direction (Uttarayan) when transitioning from Capricorn to Gemini. When moving towards the southern direction (Dakshinayan), it shifts from Cancer to Sagittarius. When it moves from one sign to another, it triggers seasonal changes as well.

Every zodiac sign plays a singular role in the changing seasons and differences in natural phenomena. For instance, while the inhibition of Aquarius and Capricorn by the Sun brings the winter season, Gemini and Taurus bring summer. The Sun's position in each zodiac sign represents the native's sun sign and can be depicted in their natal chart. The Sun can also change houses within a single zodiac sign, which can threaten the native's well-being.

The Sun and Leo

Every zodiac sign conjoins with one solitary planet in its house. In Vedic astrology, the Sun sits in the house of Leo to form a powerful entity. When the native has Leo as their zodiac sign with the Sun in its house, they tend to display strong personality traits and be well-respected in society. They can be stubborn but are quite dynamic and forceful, especially when making important decisions. They will likely be blessed with comfort and easy life. They attract immense wealth and are filled with knowledge. Also, they do not like following orders and prefer to be independent.

The Sun and Aries (Exaltation)

As mentioned, an exalted Sun displays signs of dominance, dynamism, and strength. The natives are powerful, courageous, and possess the ability to become leaders. Aries, the first zodiac sign in the series, exalts the Sun and makes it more powerful. This conjunction can greatly benefit the native. Even though the person does not wish to become the center of attention, they will still be under the spotlight thanks to their exceptional potential and skills.

The Sun and Libra (Debilitation)

Libra weakens the Sun's position and affects the natives' personal and professional lives. They may not be as successful in their careers and will likely lack effective decision-making skills. They are also prone to developing eye or skin problems, some of which are untreatable.

While a debilitated Sun is considered inauspicious, an afflicted Sun is even worse. Natives with an afflicted Sun are often ignored and never get credit for the work they do. Rahu, Ketu, Saturn, and Mars are the main planets responsible for the malefic effects and weaken a native's horoscope.

The Sun in Different Houses

As mentioned in Vedic astrology, the Sun sits in every zodiac sign's house for one month. In essence, the Sun displays the best results in almost every house. However, it can get slightly weak when entering the 4th and 7th house. The effects are aggravated when the Sun comes in contact with a weak or bad planet. As the Sun moves through the twelve houses, it projects varying effects on the native. While some are blessed with the Sun's benefic effects, others may suffer from its malefic consequences.

1st House

When the Sun is in the 1st house, the native will likely be born early in the morning. They will be tall, lean, and short-haired. Since the Sun's presence is strong in this first house, the native will be independent, strong, and possess great leadership skills. They will be stubborn, refusing to take a "no" for an answer. They will have a healthy heart, strong bones, and great overall physical health. The native is strong-willed and has excellent management skills as well. On the other hand, they may suffer from eye diseases and will probably endure a turbulent childhood.

2nd House

Individuals with the Sun in the 2nd house in their horoscope typically portray a fierce and stubborn nature. They often get into quarrels and debates. They may not be close to their family, and likely won't inherit ancestral property. The natives are directly related to the 8th house, the House of Death – and accounts for why they are blessed with longer lives. Like the first house, the natives in the second house may face adversities during childhood, specifically due to poverty and improper living conditions. These conditions can also stress and weaken them from an early age.

3rd House

As one of the most powerful placements, the Sun in the 3rd house makes for creative, strong, courageous, and confident individuals. They are inseparable from their family and will go to great lengths to protect their loved ones. Achieving wealth, fame, and respect will be some of their major achievements. They are stronger than their enemies and always win. They can communicate well and are fond of traveling. All their adventures and experiences make them wiser and more knowledgeable. In light of this, they must pursue a career in a domain related to publishing, communication, design, or public speaking. The native is at peace and enjoys their life to the fullest.

4th House

People with the Sun in this house are blessed with good memory and intelligence. They are directly related to the 10th house, so they can steadily climb up the ladder and attain higher positions in society. They work hard and believe the fruits of their labor will be visible later in life, which strengthens the core belief of delayed gratification. At some point, the native may face a major financial burden due to the loss of a vehicle, land, or house. Despite achieving success, they will constantly remain anxious due to life uncertainties and difficult childhood.

5th House

The native possesses a sharp mind but is often prone to anger. It can be difficult for them to control their temper. That said, their intelligence and sharp memory help them excel academically. Raj Yoga takes place in this house and is necessary to achieve a meaningful educational background, helping them gain an edge over their competitors. In turn, the native has a higher chance of gaining fame and becoming wealthy. The Sun manifests talent and skills, which also boosts their confidence and productivity. If the native is not careful, they may also develop overconfidence, which can be the starting point of their demise.

6th House

One of the boldest groups of all, the 6th house natives, is fierce, courageous, and physically fit. They are not afraid of their enemies and can easily spot or capture them. This phenomenon is known as "Shatruhanta Yoga," which translates to "conqueror of the enemy." With a steady life force, they can even fight diseases with ease. The Sun in this position can compel them to spend more money, *most of which is unnecessary.* The natives are unable to record their expenditures due to their questionable spending habits. Typically, the natives of the 6th house are good-looking and tend to live a comfortable life.

7th House

When the Sun is in the 7th house, the native is blessed with courage, strength, and a sharp mind. They can overcome adversities and bounce back stronger thanks to their diligence. By contrast, they can exhibit egoistic and stubborn personalities. The repercussions are visible in their marriage as they are unable to balance their personal and professional lives. Jealousy and ego also play a major role in the weakening of their relationships. Natives are often stressed and anxious. They worry about their reputation and cannot stand the idea of being publicly humiliated. A debilitated Sun can also delay the native's marriage.

8th House

The natives in this house are very curious about mystical wisdom and divert their attention toward psychic matters. This curiosity leads many to pursue careers in the occult science of astrology. They can be careless and fight over trivial matters. Natives are often found talking alone or arguing with others. Their minds are unstable, resulting in poor judgment and decision-making. A debilitated Sun can induce heart diseases and stomach-related issues – leading to a shorter lifespan. The native can also be skilled in a medical profession, which can be helpful in the future. They are highly supportive and try to help others as much as they can.

9th House

The natives in this house display signs of confidence, courage, ambition, and diligence. They are supportive and helpful individuals. The Sun's energy is strong in the 9th house, which makes them honest and virtuous. They are inclined toward spiritual energies and practice yoga or breathing exercises to tap into their authentic selves. With their helpful nature, they often partake in volunteering activities and social organizations to benefit the underprivileged. The best professions for natives are in domains such as the law, teaching, and spiritual practice. They love traveling as it feeds their hungry and curious souls.

10th House

Natives in this house want to be the center of attention in every room they step in. They will likely achieve success due to their resilience and courage and will attract fame and wealth. Their work ethic and efficiency make them the star of their workplace and inculcate leadership qualities. These career-oriented natives can become skillful managers and politicians. They want to help others and contribute to society. Many are driven by this instinct, which ultimately becomes their main motto in life. The position of the Sun in the 10th house is one of the most important placements of all due to its versatility.

11th House

The natives support truth and honesty. They are blessed with abundant knowledge and virtue. If the Sun is in an exalted position, the native will likely acquire success and fame at a young age. They respect themselves and others around them. They believe in spirituality and indulge in yoga during their free time, which is also the secret behind their strength, happiness, and exemplary well-being. Stepping into the business world is a great move as they will likely gain success as entrepreneurs. Their sources of income will be steady. However, as they age, they may develop multiple diseases and lose their stamina.

12th House

The Sun's position in the 12th house can make the native irritable, lazy, and easygoing. They often blurt out their opinions without thinking about the consequences. Their main areas of interest include paramedical science, psychic and occult studies. They are directly linked to the 6th house, which can cause harm to their enemies. Despite their friendliness, natives may not share a strong bond with their friends and loved ones. They are often perceived as indifferent and careless. As they age, they may face issues with their income and expenditure and will likely develop eye issues. However, the native will live a peaceful life and ignore all worries.

Significance of the Sun in Vedic Astrology

The Sun represents vitality, health, power, authority, soul, well-being, and ego in Vedic astrology. These concepts and values collectively define a person's soul, displaying both negative and positive traits. This is why the Sun is known as the "Atmakaraka" in Vedic astrology. The body represents our soul in its most authentic manner. Ancient worshippers offered prayers and the Sun God's favorite items during auspicious celebrations and festivals to please him. He was called "Surya Bhagwan" or "Surya Dev," Some of the festivals celebrated in his name were Samba Dashami, Makar Sankranti, and Chhath Puja. Until today, many believers still celebrate these festivals across India to please Surya Bhagwan and manifest his energy.

Nowadays, the Sun God is glorified as the main deity of many temples across India. Some of these famous temples are the Modhera Sun temple in Gujarat and the Konark Sun temple in Odisha. While other cultures view the Sun as a star, Vedic astrology calls it a planet due to its effects and repercussions on humans. In the Hindu religion, astrologers determine the Sun's position to mark its exact location in a person's horoscope. When drawing up their natal birth chart, they also determine the person's future based on the Sun's strength. If the planet is in an ideal position and exhibits strong traits, the person will be blessed with a smooth career and steady relationships. They will also have a firmer say in their personal and professional lives and will likely become leaders.

The Sun in Vimshottari Dasha

While we've already explained the Sun's significance in Vedic astrology in a previous chapter, it's important to know some lesser-known facts about the god's position in Hindu mythology. According to Hindu myths, the Sun God lived in a kingdom called Suryaloka and governed other deities. Despite being strong and powerful, the Sun is easily eclipsed by Rahu and Ketu.

On average, a person lives for 120 years. During this time, their lives are governed by the malefic and benefic effects of the nine planets, known as the "Vimshottari Dasha" or Vimshottari system. The system is further broken down into periods that determine the native's fate. The main phase is called "Mahadasha." When the Sun rules the native's Mahadasha period, they experience a phase called "Surya Mahadasha," a period lasting six years.

Every minute of a person's life is associated with a ruling planet, which helps them determine their next move. During the Sun's presence in the native's Dasha calculations, the celestial body becomes potent and establishes dominance over their life. This helps the native become socially adept and attract wealth. They are blessed with a steady source of income and can climb up the societal ladder with ease. If the Sun is placed in unfavorable houses, it can produce malefic effects such as financial losses, public humiliation, and health conditions.

The Sun as the King and Father of the Cosmic Kingdom

The fact that the Sun is stationary in the solar system while governing other planets that revolve around it showcases its significance in the cosmic kingdom. The Sun's authoritative power and masculine influence help the government or any other higher organization of the kingdom. Although the Sun manifests our soul's energy and is deeply connected to our innermost self, it still inspires us to take action and strengthen our outer shield to reach success and build a name for ourselves.

With this strength, you can overcome all shortcomings and pave the path toward your goals. Other planets respect the Sun's regal status and follow its instructions. It is the natural father of all living creatures and ensures their well-being and vitality. If your horoscope displays a strong Sun in your favor, you may possess exceptional leadership skills, be well-respected in society, and be given a higher role to portray. Individuals with a strong Sun tend to have strong bonds with their father and brother. Moreover, they will likely display signs of maturity, generosity, and dependability, especially toward the opposite gender.

On the other hand, the Sun's weak placement can affect your physical health to a major extent. Ailments like cardiovascular disease, weak eyesight, baldness, weak bones, and poor blood circulation are common with a weak Sun in one's horoscope. People may also experience a deteriorating bond with their father or any other important masculine figure in their life. What's more, natives can also suffer in their professional lives because of low self-esteem or confidence. They can be indecisive, which can affect their projects and stance within an entity. By contrast, a strong placement of the Sun can result in overly exaggerated characteristics like aggression, egoism, and even narcissism.

The Sun's Relation to the Moon in the Zodiac

In essence, the Sun sign represents a person's outer self and personality, whereas the Moon sign symbolizes their soul and inner avatar. Since they collectively represent a person's identity, the two signs are important in the zodiac system. The way both signs combine and thrive in unison determines your presence, character, and well-being. Like the Moon and the Sun co-exist in the universe, they also govern other planets and natives in harmony. However, you can still spot some rare occurrences where the Sun blocks the Moon's light and eclipses it and vice versa.

The relevance of this relationship stems from lunar phases. If both bodies sit in opposite signs, a person born under the Full Moon may be motivated to accomplish their goal or complete important missions. Ideally, both bodies trump every other aspect in our natal charts and are the primary decision-makers of our fates. The Sun governs our life's motion and supervises our progress, while the Moon ensures that we lead a secure and comfortable life. These opposing forces steer our overall well-being.

However, this can also mean that the opposing forces may create an internal conflict and confuse the native. The main interaction between both bodies depends on the varying phases of the Moon and the Sun's position. The relationship is devised in an individual's natal chart during birth. Even a minor change in the waxing or waning phase of the Moon can change a person's life, which makes us all unique and gives everyone their own "soli-lunar signature."

Chapter 4: The Conjunction of the Sun

As everyone knows, astrology allows us to track the relationships and movements between the planets and all other celestial bodies. We then use this information to analyze how these bodies affect our daily lives and our emotions, thoughts, and behaviors. If you've been reading about astrology for quite some time now, chances are you've stumbled across terms such as "square" and "trine" while looking up the description and influence of the planets. These dynamic, fast-changing correspondences are known as "aspects." In astrology, there are five major planetary aspects. They play a significant role in our understanding of how the planets and celestial bodies affect us.

So, what exactly are the aspects? When planets move through the sky in the zodiac wheel, they form angles with each other. Aspects are the description of these angles, and they all mean different things. We know that each planet rules over a specific area of our lives, and we realize that each body has acquired its own distinctive personality over time. However, how they affect us as individuals is determined by their location in the zodiac and their relationships with one another. These relationships, as mentioned, are called aspects. The five major aspects of astrology are conjunction (the topic of this chapter), sextile, opposition, square, and trine. Aspects, in short, are the behavior of the planets when they're present in different signs. It represents how each person takes general action or receives things during that time.

For instance, if two planets in the zodiac wheel are at a 0°, or close to 0°, angle of each other, this would qualify as *conjunction*. If they're at a 60° angle, then it's a sextile. To form a square, they'd have to be at a 90° angle and at 120° to form a trine. If two planets sit directly opposite each other, forming a 180° angle, this would be opposition. Every angle and aspect holds a different meaning. You can take a look at your birth chart to see a visual representation of these degrees.

Some of the five major aspects, like opposition and square, are known as hard aspects. Hard aspects bring along the more unpleasant areas of life, like struggles and challenges. The easy, or sometimes known as soft, aspects are generally positive. They handle the gentler, more favorable areas of life. The sextile and trine are considered easy aspects. A conjunction, however, doesn't belong to one or the other. The planets involved in a conjunction determine its tendency to go in either direction. Still, keep in mind that the involved planets are the real indicators, even with hard and easy aspects. Sometimes, a trine will not be in your favor, while a hard square will provide a helping hand. Expect every planetary Rendezvous to look a little different.

Needless to say, aspects are one of the basic elements of interpretations in astrology. They have the power to change each planetary placement's meaning and influence, which is why you cannot interpret just one planet in a single sign. You must also account for the other energies. Notice if two planets are co-existing harmoniously in conjunction or sitting exasperatingly in a frustrating square. Take Venus as an example. Venus is universally known as the planet of love. There are several positive nuances tied to this planet in general. However, if it's in an unfavorable aspect with Saturn, this may indicate that some difficulties will spiral in your love life.

There are various other aspects that astrologists account for in their interpretations. If you think about it, planets can exist in endless angles, creating infinite aspects. However, grasping a deeper understanding of these five major aspects is a great place to start.

As we hinted above, this chapter delves into conjunctions as an aspect. We won't be exploring just any conjunction, though. We will be exclusively exploring the conjunction of the Sun with the other planets in the same sign. You will begin to understand what makes this a very powerful astrological phenomenon and learn how it affects the various areas of your life.

What Is a Conjunction?

Since a conjunction occurs when two planets align at the same (or nearly the same) location, this aspect describes what happens when the energies of two different points or bodies blend and unite. These two points can be luminary bodies, such as Lilith and Chiron, or planets, like Earth and Jupiter. While they are not planets by definition, the Sun and the Moon do count as well.

From where we see it, points in conjunction appear to move together. They lie within the same zodiac sign, blend their energies, and act and move as one combined force. However, you still need to remember that not all blended energies are harmonious. Being in conjunction doesn't mean that two points are instantly compatible. While some of them, like Venus and the Moon, will cooperate, others like Mars and Neptune will not work together in conjunction. This is because the Moon's focus on feelings and Venus's association with love allows them to work in unison. Meanwhile, Neptune's dreamy and fantastical tendencies disrupt Mars's need for strong competition and action.

Why Does It Matter?

By understanding the locations of the planets on your birth chart, you will gather deeper insight into the universal forces that impact your personality the most. You will also be able to identify all your strongest and weakest points. Finding out which planets or bodies were in conjunction at the time of your birth can help you understand the areas of your life toward which you're most likely to direct your focus and motivation. To help you get a clearer picture, let's say Neptune, whose energy is associated with creativity, and Mercury, which is linked to communication, were both in conjunction at your birth. This would mean that you're skilled at expressing your creative ideas. It also suggests that pursuing a career in science or statistical work would put all your talents to waste.

Solar Conjunct

The celestial bodies that interact with the Sun at the time of our birth impact who we are. Its unmatchable glare makes it impossible for us to observe the planets for a few weeks, as they remain in conjunction with the sun. Harmonious unisons make way for positive changes and events. Meanwhile, the harder gatherings may pose new challenges for you, urging you to overcome several blockages.

Sun and Moon

If the Sun and the Moon were in conjunction during your birth, you might feel like you have emotionally intense and potent willpower. You can express yourself confidently, knowing that you can back and support your arguments with deep-rooted foundations. You have a heightened sense of self, making you a very subjective person; you may find it hard to relate to others or step into their shoes. You are likely a double of the zodiac that the conjunction occurs in. You are typically happy and confident in your abilities with a harmonious sextile or trine. You feel comfortable with who you are, which makes you easy to be around and form relationships with. On the other hand, you may have to deal with inner suffering if you have the challenging opposition and square. Your needs and wants can be conflicting, which makes you easily frustrated, very moody, and restless.

Sun and Mercury

These two celestial points are never more than 28° apart, creating the only conjunction. Your mind is most likely in alignment with your physical self, as Mercury is an avid interpreter for the fundamental solar drives. You probably have a natural inclination for storytelling, communication through art, music, movement (everything non-verbal), gestures, writing, and expressing your views. Since these bodies are so closely orbed, you may have a talkative, energetic personality.

Sun and Venus

Venus generally moves near the Sun, making its only solar aspect conjunction. If Venus accompanies your Sun, others may perceive you as a radiant, friendly individual. If your birth chart shows close conjunction, you may be very skilled at bringing out the beauty in various things, as well as sharing all positive aspects of life with others. You tactfully seek everything that brings you joy, pleasure and is art-related.

Sun and Mars

If this conjunction is present in your birth chart, you are probably a very energetic individual. You are dedicated when it comes to chasing your goals. You like to seize all opportunities on the spot. This conjunction, sextile, and trine show that you like to act in the heat of the moment, which makes you a rather successful person. You like to live on the edge and embrace life with open arms. You're probably over-scheduled, considering that you never say no to anything that comes your way. However, you may be prone to frustration, impulsive outbursts, anger, and rage, with a tense, hostile square. Since it can be hard to keep this intensity under control, you should consider focusing your energy on sports and physical activities.

Sun and Jupiter

If you have this combination in your birth chart, you're probably a lively, flamboyant person. You are innately generous and giving, making you an inspiring figure. You're an optimist at heart who believes in the future and all that it has in store – which can enhance your luck, further increasing your faith in the flow of things. You may also experience abundance in terms of wealth. If you have the opposition or square, you may have overly ambitious thoughts and beliefs. You may think that you can receive all the good things in life without putting in real effort. That said, if you match your innate fine attitude with self-discipline, you will finally defeat your inclination to go with the flow of life.

Sun and Saturn

If your Sun is in conjunction with Saturn, you are probably easily self-motivated. You may carry stress and pressures that only you can relieve by putting in adequate effort (as perceived by you). The trine, sextile, and conjunction of these bodies can help pave the way for you to find a basis for your natural gifts. You're generally a realist who can formulate plans to help you achieve your goals. You are a hard-working individual with high conscientiousness. You tend to set very high-performance standards for yourself, have a strong personality, and are not afraid to take on responsibilities. If you are saddled by opposition, you may feel overly burdened and weighed down. Feelings of failure may never leave you alone. However, this is something you can power through if you work hard and tolerate the frustrations.

Sun and Uranus

People with their Sun in conjunction with Uranus are blessed with an eccentric aura. Conjunction, as well as other harmonies like the sextile and trine, can make them seemingly brilliant. They are risk-takers who insist on following their unique paths. You always stand out, no matter what you choose to do. Your innovative and brilliant ideas can bring groups alive. If you have the less fortunate aspects, keep in mind that you are more likely to experience accidents, partake in high-risk behavior, and suffer from relentlessness and poor judgment.

Sun and Neptune

You are probably a very charming, almost magical individual if your birth chart's harmonies contain the combination of the Sun and Neptune. You consider your imagination one of the real world's forces, making you an artist or a dreamer. You can bring your thoughts to life, which makes you amazing at what you do. You can be very warm and giving, especially to people who seem to have lost their way, making you a memorable person and even the perfect fit for the art of healing. If you have the more challenging squares or opposition, you may end up losing sight of your own way and purpose early on.

Sun and Pluto

The harmonious aspects may impart a sense of presence, awareness, and intensity. You can easily spot out hidden information and find positivity in the things other people typically avoid. You can spiral intense emotions in those around you and have great self-confidence. You believe that people can evolve into new and improved versions of themselves. If this combination is prominent in the harder aspects, you may have an issue with power struggles. You may also feel the need to defend yourself, which can be draining. You will experience phases of destruction before you allow yourself to be renewed.

Planetary Combustion

At different points throughout the year, planets may not be visible in the sky as the Sun falls in front of them, masking them with its blazing energies. This phenomenon is called combustion and is quite a significant event in Vedic astrology. It's also one of the most difficult ones as it destroys the planets' intents and reveals their darker energies. Planetary combustion typically occurs when a planet is 2° to 3° away from the Sun, which makes sense, considering anything that gets too close to the sun ultimately gets burnt.

Vedic astrology assigns a specific distance, in degrees, to each planet. This indicates the distance at which they would combust. If the distance between the Moon and the Sun falls below 12°, the Moon would be combusted. Mars will be combusted if the distance between it and the Sun reaches below 17°. Mercury would be combusted if the distance hits below 14° and would combust at below 12° if it's in retrograde motion. If the distance is below 11°, Jupiter would be combusted. Venus would combust below 10° and under 8° if in retrograde. Finally, Saturn would combust if it hit below 15°.

Keep in mind that ancient texts include a lot of inaccurate information. This is why the majority of modern-day astrologers don't entirely trust these Vedic combustion parameters. According to today's modern research and observations, any planet will start to combust if the distance hits below 10°. If the distance becomes even shorter, at 1°, 3°, or even 5°, the planet would be officially combusted or burned. However, this is a widely controversial topic, considering that planets like Venus and Mercury are always found close to the Sun. Whether Venus and Mercury fall under the entire combustion concept is debatable.

Those two planets can get burned if they wander too close to the sun. However, they are still generally used to its heat. If they are 1° to 4° away, they will get combusted. If any planet in the zodiac becomes combusted by the Sun regardless of its initial qualities, it will lose all of its positive qualities. This means that all benevolent planets will become malicious, and the originally malicious ones will become even more detrimental. This, of course, is the case when no remedial placements are present in the zodiac.

A combusted planet can become entirely negative only if:

- It is weak in Shadbal
- It is present in a debilitated sign
- It is losing its strength in D-9
- It is below Paap Kartari yoga.

Some salvaging factors can allow planets to perform positively in the zodiac, even when they're combusted. These include:

- A combusted planet that's receiving strong benefic elements.
- Some planets, such as Mercury, Jupiter, and Venus, are highly benefic. Their beneficial elements can relieve some of the adversities of combustions.
- A combusted planet that sits in its own sign or in exaltation one in the zodiac.
- The planet can survive and will not strongly impact a certain area of your life.
- A combusted planet that occupies a house where it receives directional strength.
- The benefic planet can receive a sense of relief.
- A combusted planet that's in retrograde.
- Planets in retrograde are generally very powerful.
- A combusted planet that has good divisional chart placements, like D-60 and D-9, and is exalted.

The planet should not be weak in Shadbal for any of these alleviating factors to work.

Auspicious Yogas

According to Vedic astrology, any planet that's placed in an astrology house generates a specific outcome when it's in contact with another planet.

Raj Rajeshwar Yoga

When the Sun is in Pisces, the Raj Rajeshwar Yoga is created. Jupiter and the Moon then exist in their own sign in the natal chart, generating a solid Raj yoga. Anyone with this yoga in their natal chart has a warm and quiet personality, like the Sun and Moon, respectively. These individuals are most likely creative, respectful, and powerful. They may occupy administrative positions.

Bhaskar Yoga

When the Moon is in the 11th house away from Mercury, Mercury is in the 2nd house from the Sun, and Jupiter is in either the 9th or 5th house from the Moon, the Bhaskar Yoga situation is created. This is not a very common sight to see on a natal chart, making whoever possesses this placement an extraordinary individual. Blessed with abundance, love, and various qualities, their character will be prosperous.

Budhaditya Yoga

Because Mercury is near the Sun, it blends with it often. This powerful yoga can halt any malefic intentions of a house in a zodiac. Like Raj Yoga, Budhaditya Yoga makes brave, insightful individuals, earning them the regard and respect of the public. They are also likely to experience financial prosperity.

Vaasi Yoga

Vaasi Yoga is created whenever the Moon is in the 12th house from the Sun. Depending on how close the planets are to the Sun, this yoga can help either manifest through malicious or benefic outcomes. However, it's worth mentioning that its beneficial aspects are a lot less likely to show. In these rare instances, the individual may be sharp-minded, assertive, capable, and knowledgeable. Otherwise, while the person may be blessed with a great memory, they may face countless obstacles and may lack benevolence.

Veshi Yoga

This yoga occurs when any planet, other than the moon, exists in the 2nd house from the Sun. Like Vaasi Yoga, the proximity of the planet indicates whether there are malicious or beneficial outcomes. If a positive planet occupies the house, the individual is likely to have an appealing, attractive character. They are respectful and may hold social or political occupations. Negative placements may result in financial and business-related challenges.

Ultimately, there are various elements to consider when determining how the Sun and the other planets affect our personality. The Sun's various interactions with the different celestial bodies can leave a great impact on our lives. Now you know how the different aspects, conjunctions, and yogas affect you and everyone around you.

Chapter 5: Medical Astrology and the Sun

Medicine and astrology have had a deep-rooted connection for centuries. Ancient medical practitioners in Egypt, China, and India referred to a person's horoscope and located the position of every planet to diagnose underlying issues and ensure proper health for the patient. As the word spread across the globe, Europe joined the bandwagon of medical astrology during the medieval period, specifically around 1450-1700. They took inspiration from Arab medical astrologers and devised their own system to treat patients. In essence, several domains depended on astrology or established a symbiotic relationship to function. The medical domain, in particular, heavily depended on horoscopes, zodiac signs, and planetary movements to diagnose and treat health conditions.

Medical Aspects in Vedic Astrology

Medical astrology is considered a vital branch of Vedic astrology and has proven an effective diagnostic tool to cure diseases. Medical astrology focuses on diagnosing symptoms that lead to diseases and curing them to safeguard a person's life for a longer period. The key was to dig deeper and find the crux of the problem. Upon treating the root cause, the disease could be permanently eradicated, and the person may live a longer life. Any kind of accident or affliction caused by planetary movements may affect the native's health.

A medical astrologer finds the underlying cause of a disease by reading the native's birth chart and locating the Sun's position. Interpreting the birth chart helps them determine the person's strengths, weaknesses, approach towards health, nutritional deficiencies, and the ability to fight certain diseases. Although this process takes time, the results are quite accurate. This analysis also helps the practitioner prepare a diet chart or devise predictive methods to diminish the effects of the disease in question and approach the issue with a holistic mindset. While every planet's affliction indicates a specific disease or an issue in a specific body part, general sickness can mean that the planets are transiting in the houses and zodiac signs.

Remedial astrology is a holistic approach towards healing. It involves the practical approach or science of healing and the study of the planets and their movements in natal charts. The benefits of remedial and medical astrology are gaining traction across the globe. Medical practitioners believe that a person's treatment can be made more effective by treating the soul. Internal healing is the key to a long and healthy life, which is what medical astrology is all about. According to medical astrology, any disease or health issue should be recognized before the symptoms appear, giving the practitioner enough time to understand the problem and treat it at the core.

If the practitioner waits for the signs or symptoms to manifest, the body may be already infected with the disease, making treatment more difficult.

Medical astrologers established links between the planets and their respective organs for better reference. Planets afflict drugs, diseases, and organs, whereas zodiac signs monitor general body parts. This makes astrology a comprehensive system that governs our body and health with multiple entities in action.

This list details the ruling celestial bodies with their concerned body parts:

- **Sun:** Heart
- **Moon:** Ovaries
- **Mercury:** Respiratory System
- **Venus:** Kidneys and Reproductive System
- **Mars:** Arteries, Muscles, Hair, Nails, Teeth, and Reproductive System
- **Jupiter:** Liver
- **Saturn:** Skeleton, Bones, Skin, and Veins
- **Uranus:** Nerves, Brain, and Endocrine System
- **Neptune:** Endocrine System
- **Pluto:** Testes

Similarly, all 12 zodiac signs represent different body parts and organs. If their corresponding planets are afflicted during the conjunction, they can show signs of specific diseases or symptoms of general sickness. And while many scholars saw this association of planets and zodiac signs with organs and body parts as pure dogmas, several cultures have used logic to underpin the innuendos. According to one argument, the planets' physical characteristics can be compared to the relevant body parts to find similarities and prove the validity of the association. For example, the heat and redness emitted by Mars explain its relevance in blood circulation, muscles, and arteries.

Over time, the negative energies of planets were perceived as projections of disease and illness. If a planet failed to sit in the right house or was poorly positioned, the negative manifestation was depicted in the form of a prevalence of a disease, which had to be treated as soon as possible. Typically, a medical astrologer diagnoses a disease by preparing the patient's chart and comparing it with their birth chart. The signs and symptoms were noted to establish an approximate date of the disease's onset. During the process, astrologers found relevance between the disease and the underlying negative energies of the planets.

The Sun's Relation with the Heart

As we know, the Sun represents health and vitality. Every planet represents and governs different body parts. If a planet's position is weak, the native may incur health issues related to the body part in question. The Sun represents the heart, and its affliction can indicate a serious cardiovascular condition. It is a natural Atmakaraka that energizes the body and promotes good health. The huge star is the central governing body of the solar system, just like the heart that pumps and supplies blood to the rest of the body to carry out vital functions. When the Sun is away from the malefic effects of Rahu and Saturn, it indicates good health and overall well-being. This is why the Sun is known as the "Lord of the Heart." Alongside this, the Sun also represents the spinal cord, bone structure, stomach, brain, gallbladder, and eyes.

In parallel, the Sun monitors our digestive system and regulates blood circulation. It ensures that our body gets proper nourishment through the food we eat. Since the heart is responsible for supplying nutrients and oxygen across the body, the Sun's malefic effect can negatively affect the heart, resulting in poor blood circulation.

The Sun's Afflictions in Natal Charts

In Vedic astrology, "affliction" means negative contribution or association. When a planet is afflicted in a natal chart, it may negatively affect the native's life. Note that a weak planet is different from an afflicted planet. When the planet is weak, it can cause minor hindrances or accidents in the native's life. However, if the planet is afflicted, it can cause irreversible damage. Regardless, both states can be destructive and damaging, which is why the native must be aware of their ruling planet.

An afflicted Sun in a horoscope can result in premature baldness, poor eyesight, cardiovascular diseases, immunodeficiency, bone fractures, neuralgia, improper blood circulation, headaches, and recurring fever. Some natives may also experience anemia, polio, and joint pain. They may get headaches or feel fatigued regularly.

The Sun's position in every house can create distinct effects. For instance, if it is located in the first house, the native can suffer from health issues and poor well-being. If the Sun is placed in the 2nd, 6th, or 7th house, the native may experience problems with their family members. Typically, the following factors can help detect health issues:

- When weaker planets are located in weaker houses. For example, Rahu, Ketu, Mars, Pluto, Uranus, Neptune, and Saturn perform badly in the 12th, 8th, and 6th house
- When bad or negative aspects are projected on any planet like opposition (180°) or square (90°)
- When the Ascendant, Moon, and Sun are collectively afflicted
- When weak planets occupy certain zodiac signs such as Pisces, Scorpio, and Virgo.

It is extremely difficult to detect heart-related issues or cardiac diseases simply by looking at a person's birth chart and physical condition. However, experienced Vedic astrologers can pick points from the patient's Dasha scheme and establish a rough timeline for the illness. The following signs can help point out some unfavorable positions of the Sun in a horoscope, which can be used to detect heart issues.

- When the Sun is positioned in the 12th, 8th, or 6th house
- When the Sun is conjunct with Rahu, Ketu, Saturn, or Mars
- If it is afflicted due to a malefic association caused by the Leo sign
- If the Sun is in a debilitated state

- When the Sun is surrounded by malefic planets (also known as the Paapkartati state)
- When the 5th lord afflicts the Sun

Your astrologer can help you detect whether the Sun is weak or afflicted in your horoscope. You can also decipher the Sun's stance by recognizing certain signs, some of which include:

- Bone-related problems can indicate that the Sun is weak in your horoscope. If afflicted, the issue can turn into something more serious, like osteoporosis, which can be difficult to treat.
- A weak Sun can cause heart problems and or other serious cardiovascular issues. An afflicted Sun can mean recurring heart attacks for the native.
- A weak Sun can also result in physical disorders like blindness or deafness.
- Due to the ill effects of a weak Sun, the native will likely suffer from mental issues, mainly due to clashes and disagreements with their father.
- The native may suffer from poor eyesight or other vision-related issues, including short-sightedness or color blindness.
- Poor blood circulation and related illnesses are also common due to a weak Sun.
- Issues like stress and anxiety can be caused by low confidence, resulting from a weak Sun. This can also affect your professional life and lower your self-esteem.
- If the Sun is weak or afflicted, you may feel tired all the time. You may not be able to complete basic tasks and walk around with a limp. Your body may feel loose, and you may be easily overwhelmed.

Any of these signs can indicate that the Sun in your horoscope is either weak, inauspicious, or afflicted. Nowadays, many people suffer from heart problems and cardiovascular diseases worldwide. This is why medical astrologers suggest focusing on empowering the Sun while taking care of your body with a wholesome diet and regular physical activity.

A Holistic Approach to Better Health

Empowering the Sun and harnessing its energy has become necessary to fight heart-related diseases and maintain overall health. Doctors suggest taking a holistic approach towards building your physical and mental health with a diet and an exercise regimen favorable to the Sun and your body's vitality.

It is believed that certain medicinal plants are associated with a ruling celestial body. In the case of the Sun, plants like eyebright, rosemary, and chamomile are known to induce positive effects thanks to their color and aroma. Ayurveda suggests consuming spicy herbs like black pepper, cayenne, and cinnamon or fiery herbs like cardamom, calamus, bayberry, or saffron to harness solar energy. Practitioners also suggest using certain oils associated with the Sun's power, like eucalyptus, cinnamon, saffron, and camphor. They can be used for cooking or in aromatherapy practices as essential oils.

Other plants like Frankincense, Bergamot, Bay Laurel, Juniper Berry, Neroli, Carrot, Angelica, Motherwort, Rosemary, Ginger, and Mandarin are good for the heart and improving blood circulation. Since some of these plants depend on the Sun's energy and light to grow, they can turn their malefic effects into beneficial ones. Growing these plants in your garden can also help improve your memory and make you more knowledgeable.

In the past, medical practitioners did not understand the chemical composition of medicinal herbs and plants. They referred to the plants' shape, size, and color to determine their potency, a dependency known as the "doctrine of correspondences." According to the practitioners, God had inscribed a pattern and elaborated a system to decipher the effectiveness of each plant. These signs were based on hidden features and textures that helped distinguish the types to treat specific diseases. For example, doctors used red herbs to treat hemorrhages and fevers and yellow flowers for liver problems. Even if the herbs did not do much to treat the issue, they were still incorporated in the treatment.

Still, practitioners realized early on the importance of a good and healthy diet for internal healing. Your doctor can help you prepare a diet plan that will not only be good for your heart and brain but also promote better overall health. Incorporate foods that are good for your heart, like berries, jaggery, almonds, whole grains, beans, walnuts, green leafy vegetables, and other items rich in Omega-3 fatty acids. Needless to say, the food you eat can help cleanse your internal system and fight free radicals, which can otherwise pose a threat to your health.

Vedic astrologers suggest practicing these habits every day to counteract the effects of an afflicted Sun:

- Fast once a week, preferably on Sundays.
- Chant the mantra, "Om hram hreem hroum sah suryaya namah," a few times every day. The native should complete 6,000 chants within 40 days.
- Chant the Gayatri mantra, "Om bhur bhuvah svah, tat savitur varenyam, bhargo devasya dhimahi, dhiyo yo nah prachodayat" a few times a day.
- Donate sugar candy and wheat to the underprivileged once a week, preferably on Sundays.

According to Vedic astrology, some common remedies and healing tips in everyday life include:

- Performing Surya Namaskar twice a day, especially in the morning. This yoga practice is also good for your heart and overall health. It promotes flexibility and boosts concentration.
- Wearing orange or yellow-colored outfits.
- Using "Ek Mukhi Rudraksha" to reduce the Sun's ill effects and attract its positive energy.
- Wearing gold in the form of rings, necklaces, and pendants.

- Incorporating yellow-colored foods in your diet.
- Wearing a ring with a real ruby gemstone. Consult an experienced astrologer before taking this step, as you must wear it on auspicious days. It is also important to focus on the placement and the type of metal you are using.
- Using a copper pot to offer water in the direction of the Sun every morning. This is the best way to start your day on a positive note and absorb those bright, cheerful sun rays that can improve your health. It also helps alleviate stress up to an extent.
- Meditating every day and practicing breathing exercises. Meditation is the best way to calm yourself down and release stress. It clears your mind and provides energy. To attract positive vibrations, chant "Om Suryaya Namaha" 108 times while meditating. If possible, pick a spot outdoors to absorb sun rays in the morning.
- Attaching a Bel tree root to a white thread and wearing it around your neck. This can reduce the negative impact of a malefic Sun. You can also tie a Baelmool root in a pink cloth and place it on your waist or arm. If possible, place the bundle in your pocket early in the morning on a Sunday as the Sun aligns with the Uttarshada, Uttarphalguni, and Kritika Nakshatras.
- Drinking water from a copper glass or bowl.

These remedies will likely reduce the Sun's malefic effects and promote a healthier life. If turned into habits, some of these practices can also encourage self-improvement in relation to your personal and professional life.

How Can Homeotherapy Help?

The health benefits of homeotherapy (like homeopathy) are applied to the spiritual teachings of astrology, giving rise to a discipline called "Astro-homeopathy." The astrological readings can detect underlying conditions in a person, whereas homeotherapy can be used to treat the issue at its core. The idea is to extract every deep-seated problem to ensure that they do not occur again, which is also the main goal of homeotherapy. Although it may take some time, the investment is worthwhile as the results are long-lasting.

Aside from consuming a nutritious diet and following homeotherapy, doctors suggest exercising regularly to keep your heart healthy. Even a 30-minute daily walk can improve your heart health and oxygen flow. Other cardiovascular exercises include running, swimming, playing sports, and aerobics. These exercises also help strengthen your bones and joints as well. Since a weak Sun in your horoscope can also cause joint or bone-related conditions, regular exercise can diminish these ill effects. Consult your doctor or a trained fitness instructor to get a customized exercise plan based on your body type and underlying health issues.

Chapter 6: Sun Signs: Aries to Cancer

In astrology, the Sun represents, among many things, the conscious ego. All the other planets revolve around it, and they reflect the workings of our subconscious mind. Western astrology sun signs are Aries, Taurus, Gemini, Cancer, Leo, Virgo, Libra, Scorpio, Sagittarius, Capricorn, Aquarius, and Pisces. Knowing these twelve signs can help astrologers learn more about a person's personality and the meaning behind their birth chart, which shows the locations of the planets. In this chapter, we set out to explore the Sun signs from Aries to Cancer. You'll get a brief overview of each Sun sign, the element and polarity it belongs to, the characteristics of each sign, the symbols behind them, and the perspective between Western astrology vs. Vedic astrology for each sign.

Aries: The Ram

Aries is a fire sign with the qualities of energy, strength, aggressiveness, spontaneity, courage, and pioneering spirit. People who fall under the Aries Sun sign are creative, confident, and independent. They have great ambitions and goals in life. Putting themselves out there comes naturally for them because they like to be the center of attention.

Aries is ruled by the planet Mars, which symbolizes energy, strength, and power. Aries is a masculine sign, so it's associated with fire like all other masculine signs. The Sun stays in Aries from March 21 to April 19. This sign is also associated with the first house because it comes at the beginning of the Zodiac, symbolizing the start of a new cycle. Aries belongs to the group of signs marking the beginning of a new year. Other signs that fall in this category are Leo, Cancer, Libra, and Capricorn.

Element

Aries belongs to the element of fire, like all masculine signs. Being a fire sign, it prefers action instead of words. These people are very enthusiastic and passionate about their goals. However, they may lose interest quickly if no immediate progress is made toward their said goal. They hate to waste time on tasks that do not involve action or anything productive. They enjoy being in constant movement, always on the move. They are also impulsive because they act immediately without thinking twice about it.

Polarity

Aries is a positive polarity sign, so Aries is usually an upbeat sign that likes to stay active and busy. However, the polarity changes when their energy turns negative because they are quick-tempered and impatient. This makes it difficult for them to work with others who have opposite views and opinions in life.

Symbols

The symbol of Aries is the ram. The ram's head is a very prominent feature since it represents its impulsive and quick-tempered nature. Also, another common visual for this sign is the fire that comes out of its horns or head, showing how generous and warmhearted they are because they bring light and warmth to the people around them.

In Western astrology, the symbol for this planet is a circle with an arrow pointing outwards. The circle represents the Sun and its ability to make things grow. The arrow represents Mars, which rules Aries, symbolizing how these individuals excel at progressing towards their goals and making things happen instead of letting them stagnate.

In Vedic astrology, the planetary symbol for Aries is a ram's head. It also has two arrow-like horns, signifying its ability to produce results quickly and take action immediately without hesitation. The type of energy represented by this sign can be seen through the ram's head because it moves around frantically, looking for new things to do.

Characteristics

The symbolism and meaning behind Aries make it clear what kind of character they tend to have. They are active, enthusiastic people who are always on the move and looking for new things to keep them busy. They prefer being in movement because it makes them feel alive. If you know someone who has the Aries Sun sign, you'll notice how enthusiastic they are and how much energy they have. Aries is also known to be very confident and independent. They have high ambitions in life, and they are always up and running, trying to make progress towards their goals. However, Aries can sometimes act impulsively because they tend to move with haste. If this becomes a negative aspect for them, it could lead to negative outcomes in life.

Taurus: The Bull

Taurus is associated with the second house in astrology as it follows Aries, making it the second sign of Spring. Taurus is responsible for providing food and shelter to humans. The Sun stays in Taurus for approximately two and a half months in the northern hemisphere, lasting from April 20th to June 21st.

The ruling planet of Taurus is Venus, the goddess of love and beauty. People born under this sign are usually attractive, warmhearted people who appreciate the beauty in life and nature.

They have a great appreciation for the finer things and enjoy taking pleasure from them. They can be quite stubborn at times because they will refuse to change their views due to their strong opinions.

Element

Taurus is one of the three earth signs, along with Virgo and Capricorn. Earth signs are naturally caring people who have a great understanding of the depth of life. It also helps that they have an excellent sense of taste because they enjoy eating delicious food whenever possible. They also love to be surrounded by aesthetically pleasing things. Being an earth sign, they love anything physical like art and music. They are creative and sensual. Taurus are very artistic people and possess a love for beauty. They appreciate good food, nice clothes, and beautiful art pieces. Taurus is also known to be patient and reliable because they do not like changing their routine or doing anything spontaneously.

Polarity

In Western astrology, Taurus is considered to be masculine or positive. In Vedic Astrology, Taurus is a feminine sign that has both positive and negative qualities. It can act like a masculine sign in some cases because of its dominance and the way it makes decisions without consulting anybody else. However, it also possesses many feminine traits, such as sensitivity and affection. It is also capable of caring for other people, which makes it a very balanced sign.

Symbols

In Western Astrology, the symbol for Taurus is a bull's head facing to the left, representing how Taurus subjects focus on providing for their family and ensuring that all responsibilities are taken care of as efficiently as possible. The second half of the symbol, which is a man's face looking to his left, represents Taurus's natural polarity. This also shows that they are in tune with other people's emotions and can tell when somebody is upset or sad.

In Vedic astrology, the symbol for Taurus is a bull lying down on its side. It has two sharp horns and a one-pointed hoof. The bull represents Taurus's stability and power while lying down on its side shows how passive it can be in nature.

Characteristics

Taureans are known to be grounded individuals who possess a realistic perspective. You can expect them to be practical and pragmatic about the things they encounter throughout their lives. One might even say that they are overly practical because they cannot just sit back and enjoy the moment. Instead, they analyze things and try to figure out their flaws, no matter how much time or energy it takes them. They need something tangible to enjoy themselves properly, which means a lot of patience is needed by others if somebody wants them to be spontaneous every once in a while.

Taurus natives are also known to be stubborn, which means they do not like it when anybody tries to tell them what to do. They prefer making their own decisions and doing things their way. As long as you let them live their lives how they see fit, you will have no problems with them. Taurus will usually not interfere in other people's business, and they expect the same of others in return. They try to be sensible and reasonable because they know that dealing with people in their daily lives is necessary.

Gemini: The Twins

The third sign of the zodiac is Gemini or The Twins. Those born under this sign are considered quick-witted and very outgoing. They love to talk about anything and everything. They are intelligent and possess a great sense of humor. They can easily adapt to any environment because they love making new friends and meeting new people. Gemini is the only sign with two different personalities, meaning they act differently depending on who they are with. It is also the only sign that has a set of twins represented in its symbol. The Sun stays in Gemini for approximately two and a half months, from May 21 to July 20.

Element

Geminis belong to the element of air, thanks to their intellectual mind and quick-thinking skills when it comes to situations where logic is needed. They are very social people, which is why the element of fire would not suit their personality. Fire needs a lot of energy and excitement to keep going, whereas Gemini thrives on information and communication to make them feel alive.

Polarity

Gemini is considered a masculine and positive sign in Western astrology, while, in Vedic astrology, it is feminine with both positive and negative traits. It is masculine when it comes to how they make decisions and the way they show leadership. They are independent and rational thinkers, which can sometimes cause problems with other people because of their habit of questioning everything. On the other hand, Gemini can sometimes be very emotional. These negative traits stem from the fact that they do not always make decisions based on reason and logic. They tend to let their emotions get the better of them, which is why they can prove unpredictable at times.

Symbols

Gemini's polarity shows up in its symbol as well. The Western astrology version portrays two human figures facing each other, whereas the Vedic version has a human figure facing forward with another human figure facing to the side. This symbolizes Gemini's ability to adapt and adjust easily in any kind of environment. The symbol also showcases how peaceful they are by having both figures hold hands, which signifies friendship.

Characteristics

Geminis can be quite charming as people, but not always sweet and innocent. They can also be very selfish at times, acting out whenever they do not get what they want. That is why those unlucky enough to get close to Geminis should be prepared for anything because they will never know what goes on in their minds or how they will react until they have already done something. They are an unpredictable group who can turn into very dangerous enemies if you happen to get on their bad side.

Cancer: The Crab

One of the most emotional signs of the zodiac, Cancer, is also very intuitive and perceptive about their surroundings. They are deep thinkers and have a habit of analyzing everybody they encounter. This can come off as being judgmental or acting stuck-up because their nature is a little snobby – not because they think they are better than everyone else, but because Cancerians want to know someone's motives before befriending them. They do not take things at face value and look for deeper meanings in anything that people say. Since Cancer believes in staying positive all the time, they will only see the negative side of things if they are extremely upset. The Sun stays in Cancer from approximately June 21 to July 22.

Element

Cancer belongs to the element of water because it is a very emotional and unpredictable sign that can often be hard to read. They can be positive or negative depending on the situation, which means when something bad happens, they tend to overreact. On the other hand, when something good happens, they are ready to celebrate and will be extremely happy about it. Cancer's element also explains their sensitivity towards others since water is a very empathetic element that feels things deeply instead of air, which can detach itself from emotions more easily.

Polarity

Cancer is considered a feminine and positive sign in Western astrology, while in Vedic astrology, it is also feminine with both positive and negative traits. It is masculine when it comes to their strength and desire to protect themselves from anything they consider harmful, such as emotional pain or people who want to hurt them physically. They are excellent at storing up information from the past and using it to protect themselves at the right time. They will try to figure out the other person's motives before they say or do anything because they fear being tricked or taken advantage of.

Symbols

The Crab is considered Cancer's symbol in Western astrology, while the lotus flower represents it in Vedic astrology. The Crab refers to Cancer's desire to protect itself from harm, while the lotus flower signifies life and purity since they have an extremely high pain tolerance. The thorny stem represents their ability to withstand physical pain, while the beautiful flowers symbolize their strong emotions that are on display for all to see.

Characteristics

Trying to figure out how a Cancerian thinks or feels can prove difficult due to their mysterious nature. Not only are they afraid of being tricked or taken advantage of, but they also have a hard time trusting other people with their true feelings. They would rather keep things bottled up inside because it is easier than exposing themselves and dealing with the consequences afterward, such as embarrassing themselves if they do not feel the same way. Although Cancerians are sensitive individuals, they hide their emotions behind a tough exterior armor because they do not want to seem weak in front of others. Ultimately, Cancer is an introverted sign that does not like getting involved with things unless they can gain something from the situation. Their emotions are extremely volatile, and they do not want to show anyone how weak their heart truly is because they fear that people will use it against them.

In this chapter, we have covered the Sun's journey from Aries to Cancer and have explained what each sign means for a particular native. We have considered both Western astrology and Vedic astrology to get a better understanding of the nature of these signs.

We discussed Aries, the first sign of the Zodiac, to Cancer, the fourth sign of the Zodiac. We talked about Aries' fire element and how it belongs to a masculine quality because there is no such thing as going too far or being soft. The symbol for Aries is a ram, and its characteristics are leading rather than following impulsiveness and the willingness to fight.

We then discussed Taurus, the second sign of the Zodiac. Its element is Earth, while its polarity is feminine, and it is considered a negative sign in Vedic astrology. The symbol for Taurus is a bull, and its characteristics are persistence, possessiveness, patience, reliability. After that, we talked about Gemini, which belongs to the air element yet also possesses masculine characteristics. Its element is dualistic due to the balance between ideas, thoughts, and communication found within this sign. Gemini's symbol is the twins, and its characteristics are being disorganized, impatient, and superficial. Lastly, we talked about Cancer who belongs to water but is considered negative by Vedic astrology. Its element is emotion, and it has feminine characteristics. Cancer's symbol is the crab, and its characteristics involve inquisitiveness, hiding their emotions, suspicion, and worrying too much.

Chapter 7: Sun Signs: Leo to Scorpio

As we've seen, Sun signs in Astrology represent the personality of an individual. The position and movement of the Sun across the sky at different points throughout their lives give insight into their character traits, how they interact with others, and their level of energy. In this chapter, we will be covering the Sun signs from Leo to Scorpio. You'll discover the elements, characteristics, symbolism, and effects of the Sun's transit in the Leo, Virgo, Libra, and Scorpio signs.

Leo: The Lion

Leo represents strength, pride, nobility, royalty, and leadership. Ruled by the Sun, Leo natives tend to have magnetic personalities and are often imposing in stature. Their personality is characterized by being a natural-born leader who longs for the limelight and enjoys praise from others. The Sun stays in Leo for around two months, from mid-July to mid-September.

Element

Leo, represented by Fire in Western astrology, and heat or energy flow within Vedic Astrology, is associated with the Sun. Fire signs tend to be energetic, warm, lively, and adventurous. They take the initiative and pursue a leadership role in most situations. As they blaze through life, they inspire others to act quickly and are generally good communicators. There is a strong presence with those born under fire signs as their fiery personalities can leave others blown away.

The element of Fire is associated with action, boldness, and passion. Fire signs tend to be confident in their actions and decisions. They are self-motivated people who move quickly once they've settled on doing something. According to Western astrology, Fire tends to have an outgoing, energetic nature associated with extraversion.

Polarity

Leo is a masculine sign in Western astrology, which is why it is associated with the Sun. The Sun represents masculinity and vitality. The priority for men with strong Leo energy is to make their presence known and noticed by others. Men may struggle with feeling prideful or arrogant at times, but they ultimately strive to be recognized as confident and powerful leaders.

Women with strong Leo energy usually come across as warm and confident. They use their charm, charisma, and other people-centric skills to draw others towards them. Their attitude generally says, "The world revolves around me," coupled with a sense of pride or arrogance that can attract or repel those in their lives, depending on how it comes across.

Symbols

The Lion is a common symbol for those with the Sun in Leo. It represents strength, pride, and courage. People with the Sun on Leo present the trait of strength represented by the king of the jungle, who is meant to be powerful. They like being in control and having authority over others. Although they have warm personalities, they can be intimidating with their authoritative presence.

The Lion also represents leadership and royalty. Those born under the Leo sign are natural-born leaders who aim to exercise control in most situations, whether in business or at home. They aren't afraid to take charge when necessary and inspire others through their confidence and self-assuredness.

Characteristics

People with Sun in Leo tend to have magnetic personalities and take pride in their appearance. They enjoy attention from others who can appreciate their confidence, charm, and charisma. Those born under this sign are not always concerned about their emotions or how they come across to others, as long as they receive praise. They like being recognized for their accomplishments and love feeling appreciated by others.

Emotions are not always a priority for those with Sun in Leo as they tend to be more goal-oriented. They want to have their presence known and feel most confident when they're the center of attention or at least know that everyone has good things to say about them. If someone does not admire them or says something negative about them, it can affect their mood and leave them feeling empty until they receive validation again.

Virgo: The Virgin

Virgo rules over earth and is considered feminine in Western astrology. Those with this position of the Sun tend to strive for perfection, both in their looks and actions. They are concerned about how they appear to others and strive to achieve a clean-cut, orderly lifestyle that reflects their attention to detail. The Sun stays in Virgo from August 23 to September 22. People born under this sign tend to be perfectionists with a very critical eye, whose approach can sometimes result in self-criticism. They are natural analysts who want absolute control over their surroundings, leading them to become workaholics or overachievers. Those with strong Virgo energy may struggle with feeling insecure at times but tend to be hard on themselves, compared to others.

Element

Virgo is an earth sign. People born under this sign can seem shy and reserved, but they're very observant when it comes to human nature. These individuals are down-to-earth and practical people who can easily move past their emotions as they tend to be more focused on the physical world. They have a good sense of reality and can clearly see the world despite distractions or anything interfering with their perception. They understand things on a deeper level due to their acute way of thinking, making them good problem-solvers and critical thinkers.

Polarity

Virgo is a feminine sign in Western astrology. Those born under this sign are balanced between their masculine and feminine energies, where they tend to be more nurturing and supportive of others, especially those who are struggling. Despite their strong need for control, Virgos don't take advantage of people's vulnerabilities. If someone is down on their luck, those with this sign are the first to lend a helping hand to help them to pick themselves back up again. People will open up to them because they can relate thanks to their shared experiences.

By contrast, in Vedic Astrology, Virgo is masculine. Those born under this sign are very much concerned about their desires and how to fulfill them. They make decisions based on what they think will benefit them the most, even if it comes at the expense of others. Those with a masculine Virgo Sun may become workaholics to avoid dealing with their emotions.

Symbols

The symbol for Virgo is the Virgin. Those with this zodiac sign may be well-known as hopeless romantics due to their desire for perfection in a partner. They would rather stay single than settle for someone who doesn't have all of their desired qualities, regardless of how amazing they might be otherwise. In Vedic astrology, Virgo's symbol is a woman holding sheaves of corn. In Western astrology, the symbol for Virgo is a young maiden holding an ear of wheat. She is thought to be either Astraea or Ceres due to these associations with the goddesses of virginity and motherhood.

Characteristics

People with this position of the Sun are more compassionate towards others than they are towards themselves. They prefer to look out for others instead of pursuing their own needs and wants. Virgos will often sacrifice what they want to help someone else without expecting anything in return. There may be times when people born under this sign feel taken advantage of, but they will continue to offer help and support, knowing that it's necessary. They may come across as perfectionists because they want everything in their own lives to be perfect. They will often hone themselves down to a fine point to continue moving towards their goal of success and wealth.

Libra: The Scales

Those born with the Sun in Libra tend to be communicators who enjoy having a large social circle. They can become restless when they're alone for too long, so they need to maintain harmony throughout their relationships. The Sun stays in Libra from September 23 to October 22. Libras are easy-going but often have a hidden agenda. They want to maintain balance and peace in their lives at all times, which may prompt them to be passive-aggressive or even manipulative when they feel like things aren't going their way.

Element

Libra is an air sign. Those born under this sign tend to be intellectual, communicative, and social people. They are good at getting things done effectively to achieve their goals without creating any conflict or drama. They tend to be fair-minded and like to see both sides of a story before forming an opinion, which helps them come up with a final verdict that everyone can be happy with. People born under this sign can seem to be indecisive, but they're simply weighing the pros and cons of their choices to make an informed decision.

Polarity

Libra is a feminine sign in Western astrology. Those born under this sign are understanding and supportive of those who are struggling. They have a keen sense of justice which compels them to stand up and speak out when they see someone being mistreated. Even though Libras can be seen as observers, it doesn't mean they aren't passionate about things that matter to them. They prefer to listen rather than speak, making it easier for them to maintain a sense of harmony in their relationships.

In Vedic astrology, Libra is a masculine sign. Those born under this sign are more concerned with getting things done rather than spending time planning and strategizing. They have little patience for indecisiveness and will take the bull by the horns whenever possible. They enjoy being physically active and like to maintain an active lifestyle because they get bored easily.

Symbols

The astrological sign of Libra is the scales, symbolizing justice and fairness, which may be why Libras tend to be aware of their surroundings, especially when it comes to social dynamics. They know when something isn't right with a friend, lover, or colleague and will do what they can to fix it.

In Vedic astrology, the sign of Libra is linked to the serpent, symbolizing resurrection and purity, which gives insight into a Library's tendency to cleanse themselves of negative habits to start afresh. In Western astrology, the sign of Libra is also associated with the phoenix that symbolizes rebirth and renewal.

Characteristics

Librans are known to be gentle, tactful, and agreeable people. They work hard to maintain balance in their lives so they can achieve their goals through non-violent means. Even though Librans may appear to be passive or even reserved at times, this is merely a facade that hides their strong yet hidden willpower. They can be shy at first but won't let that stop them from making their interests known.

Scorpio: The Ruler of the 8th House

Those born with the Sun in Scorpio tend to be emotional people who are very protective of themselves and their loved ones. They will do whatever it takes to take care of those closest to them, leading them to become obsessive or possessive at times. The Sun stays in Scorpio from approximately October 23 – November 22.

Element

Scorpio is a water sign. Those born under this sign are very intuitive individuals who can delve deep into the minds of those around them. People with this position of the Sun know what motivates someone before they even say anything, and it helps them form better and more accurate opinions about people.

Polarity

Scorpio is a feminine sign in Western astrology. Those born under this sign do whatever they can to maintain their independence and freedom by keeping those around them at arm's length. They are very private individuals who guard their emotions fiercely, making it hard for others to approach them, let alone see beyond the surface.

In Vedic astrology, Scorpio is a masculine sign. Those born under this sign are more intensely focused than Libras, which can be off-putting for people who don't understand their motivations. They tend to overreact when they feel threatened and make it difficult for others to get close to them and form any kind of real connection.

Symbols

The astrological symbol for Scorpio is the scorpion which represents sex, death, and rebirth. People with this sign in their astrological chart tend to hold very strong emotions and passions beneath the surface. They spend a lot of time pondering these thoughts but don't often share them with others, which leaves people intrigued by what could be going on in their minds.

In Vedic astrology, Scorpio is linked to the eagle, which symbolizes spiritual wisdom and enlightenment. With this sign, the person will tend to be a deep thinker who spends a lot of time contemplating life and its place within it. They constantly ask themselves why they do certain things and how they can do them better, giving them an eye for detail when analyzing habits and behaviors.

Characteristics

Those born with the Sun in Scorpio tend to be very passionate and intense people who aren't afraid of expressing what they have to say. They can come across as domineering or aggressive, but their actions are typically rooted in a desire to protect themselves and those around them from harm. This sign is thought to correspond closely with magic, which is one reason why these people are often drawn to the occult. People born under this sign aren't afraid to take risks if they feel that taking them will make their life better, even if it means failing miserably at them in the end.

This chapter covered the Sun signs from Leo to Scorpio. It explained elements for each sign, the masculine and feminine characteristics of each sign, symbols for the signs, and the traits of each Sun sign. Starting with Leo, the Sun stays in this sign from July

23 - August 22. This is a fire sign which means those born under it are very energetic people who easily display their emotions. Leo is considered a masculine sign in Western astrology, but it is seen as a feminine one in Vedic astrology. When it is in Leo, the symbol for the Sun is the Lion symbolizing power, royalty, and strength. A person born under this sign will be very proud and often need admiration from others. However, they are equally as capable of giving it.

We then discussed the Sun sign Virgo, a feminine earth sign (females are more common than males) that resides in the Sun sign Virgo from August 23 - September 22. In Western astrology, this sign is considered masculine, and in Vedic astrology, the Sun stays in this sign for two months, meaning both genders are candidates for this Sun sign. The symbol for Virgo is the Virgin with a sheaf of wheat signifying work and harvest. People born under this sign will often be hard workers who never seem to take a break from their tasks because they like to finish what they start. They are down-to-earth and practical people who display their emotions less freely than others.

Next, we talked about Libra, which the Sun resides in from September 23 - October 22. It is considered a masculine sign in Western astrology, while it is considered a feminine Sun sign in Vedic astrology. The symbol for Libra is the scales, symbolizing equality. This is an air sign meaning that those born under it are quite introspective and intellectual people who spend a lot of time contemplating their inner thoughts and feelings rather than expressing them. Those with their Sun in this sign are fair-minded people who like to come up with creative solutions to difficult problems for the benefit of all.

Lastly, after Libra, we discussed Scorpio. This is a water sign, meaning that those born under it are emotional and often secretive people who prefer to keep their thoughts and feelings to themselves. In Western astrology, it is considered a feminine sign, while in Vedic astrology, the Sun stays in this sign for two months so both genders can claim Scorpio as their Sun sign. The symbol for Scorpio is the scorpion which symbolizes sex, death, and rebirth. People with their Sun in this sign are passionate people with a lot of intensity inside, and they can also be very intense lovers.

Chapter 8: Sun Signs: Sagittarius to Pisces

By now, it goes without saying that the Sun is the life of all living things on Earth. And while it won't live forever, its positive effects are felt by all who walk upon and inhabit this planet. The Sun occupies Sagittarius, Capricorn, Aquarius, and Pisces from November 21 until April 18. These four signs are different as they belong to two separate planets, Jupiter and Saturn. In this chapter, you'll discover the elements, characteristics, symbolism, and effects of the Sun's transit in these four signs.

Sagittarius: The Minister and Advisor

Sagittarius is an optimistic, honest, confident, and free-spirited fire sign. Sagittarians are straightforward people with a great sense of humor. They're often blunt in their thoughts but can also be philosophical and frank when it comes to the truth about themselves or others. These people have high principles, and their code of ethics is important to them. They're excellent advisers and messengers thanks to their good judgment, strong intuition, and to have a great sense of direction. A Sagittarius can achieve success in many areas due to their optimism and enthusiasm for life.

Saturn is considered the enemy of the Sun, whereas Jupiter is seen as his minister and advisor. In Sagittarius, which belongs to Jupiter, the Sun represents happiness and optimism. As it travels through this sign, it gives humans a love for adventure and a need for freedom. The positive effects of the Sun when it occupies Sagittarius can help the native feel less inhibited and more willing to take risks. The Sun in Sagittarius allows you to see life as an adventure, learn from your past, focus on the path ahead, and feel great about yourself.

Element

The Sagittarius sign belongs to the element of fire and is ruled by Jupiter. Sagittarians are envied by many for their optimism, honesty, confidence, and great sense of humor, as well as their high principles. The element of fire is positive as it represents warmth and inspiration. According to Vedic astrology, the fire element is associated with both energy and transformation. Fire rules the emotions, so Sagittarians need to remember that they need to take care of themselves emotionally to avoid stress or burning out.

Symbol

The symbol for the Sagittarius sign is the centaur. Centaurs are mythical creatures with the head, arms, and torso of a human and a horse's body, legs, and tail. This creature represented freedom to roam any land since they could run on both lands and in water. The centaur was known to be half-man, half-animal in both its human and horse features. This symbolizes the need for humans to find a balance between their spiritual and animalistic sides. The Sagittarius symbol is a centaur because this sign represents freedom and optimism. The Sagittarian finds a sense of balance through action rather than meditation.

Characteristics

Sagittarians are straightforward and frank when it comes to the truth. They are excellent advisers and messengers as they generally have strong intuition and a great sense of judgment and direction.

They're optimistic and enthusiastic about life, which allows them to achieve success in many areas. They tend to be honest with themselves about their feelings and needs, while others can sometimes struggle with this. These people need to remember that they must take care of themselves emotionally to avoid finding themselves in insufferable situations.

Effects

As the Sun travels through the Sagittarius sign, it reminds humans to embrace adventure and preserve their freedom. Sagittarians are more willing to take risks because optimism and enthusiasm are present in their life. The negative effects of the Sun when it occupies Sagittarius can cause the native to be blunt, sometimes offensive, without thinking about how this may affect others.

Capricorn: The Mountain Goat

In Capricorn, which belongs to Saturn, the Sun represents a drive for power, authority, and ambition. When going through this sign, the Sun can cause humans to be obsessed with achieving their goals and destroying anything that gets in their way. When the Sun leaves Sagittarius and enters Capricorn on December 22, those born under these signs will find themselves drawn to power and authority. They will also feel a strong need to prove themselves capable of achieving their goals.

Element

The Capricorn sign belongs to the element of earth and is ruled by Saturn. Capricorns are hardworking, responsible, patient, and trustworthy people with a strong desire for success. They're skilled at using their mind and determination to achieve what they set out to do. The earth element is positive as it represents reliability and strength of will. According to Vedic astrology, the element of earth is associated with both the aforementioned traits and realism. In Western astrology, earth rules over stability and materialism.

Symbol

The Capricorn symbol is a mountain goat because this sign represents both leadership and ambition. Capricorns are hardworking people who constantly seek to improve their lives while staying practical about achieving their goals. The mountain goat is, in fact, an excellent climber and leader. This sign can lead others while standing on top of a mountain peak facing downward toward their subjects. This represents both leadership and ambition and the need for Capricorn natives always to be goal-oriented to succeed.

Characteristics

The Capricorn sign has an emotional depth and is passionate about life. The Sun moving through Capricorn can cause those born under this sign to become more responsible, serious, ambitious, and focused on their goals. This can also affect the way they see themselves, as they may be drawn to a materialistic world with many opportunities to achieve success even at an early age.

Capricorn is a cardinal sign and is the most ambitious of all Earth signs. Being ambitious means that this sign has an unwavering desire to achieve their goals and become successful in life at all costs. The symbol for this sign is the mountain goat, representing a hardworking, responsible person who focuses on setting and achieving their objectives. A Capricorn native has a natural sense of leadership and is very goal-oriented.

Effects

The Sun in Capricorn can cause people to gain better focus while becoming obsessed with achieving their goals. The negative effects of the Sun when it moves through Capricorn are that these natives can become obsessive, controlling, and insensitive towards others. They will work restlessly until they have reached a certain level of success, which explains why this sign tends to be more ambitious than others.

Aquarius: The Water Bearer

In Aquarius, which belongs to Saturn, the Sun represents a desire for knowledge, higher learning, and new ideas. These individuals can teach others and use their minds to advance themselves further to achieve success. When the Sun moves through this sign from December 22 until January 20, it enters the last third of Saturn's territory, which will compel those born under this sign to become more ambitious. Aquarians will find themselves drawn to radically new concepts and ideas, especially when they go against the norm. These people will also feel a strong need to break free from anything that makes them feel trapped or restrained.

Aquarians are considered some of the most unpredictable people in the zodiac because they don't like to follow conventions and rules. They aren't too concerned with what others think of them and would rather trust their emotions. Natives of this sign often have a strong sense of social responsibility and can be very helpful to those around them. They're known for their friendliness, and they tend to think of others before themselves.

Element

In Western astrology, the element of air is associated with both science and philosophy. Air rules over intelligence and memory as well as communication. The water element, on the other hand, represents emotions and intuition. In Vedic astrology, Jupiter (the son of Saturn) rules the element of water. Water rules over intelligence and imagination. The Aquarius symbol is a man pouring water from two pitchers to represent both the thirst for knowledge and the desire to share that knowledge.

Symbol

The Aquarius symbol is the Water Bearer as it represents one who can control life's most powerful forces, including water. The Sun rules over all fiery energy, and fire represents both wisdom and passion. This is why the Sun in Aquarius can push natives to be intelligent, insightful, emotionally sensitive, and introverted. In Vedic astrology, the symbol for Aquarius is the Great One. It represents a desire to achieve greatness or success.

Characteristics

People born under the Aquarius sign are helpful, calm, and friendly. They love to be around others but can also be introverted at times when feeling overwhelmed by their emotions. These natives do not like to stay in one place for too long and prefer exploring new things as often as they can. They're extremely intelligent and like to stay educated on a variety of subjects. Aquarians are also sympathetic and giving, but they can be distant when it comes to relationships.

Aquarius individuals don't like to get involved in things that make them feel overly emotional. They're not overly concerned with their image and the opinions others have about them, meaning they don't let things get to their head. Aquarius natives also hate being controlled, so they don't let money have power over them. These people are highly intelligent and can be excellent teachers. Aquarians are known to be rebellious and can see difficult concepts in a new light. They are also creatives at heart, which means they may have great imaginations and easily develop new ideas.

Aquarius is a fixed sign, meaning these individuals are loyal and stable. Being ruled by Saturn, they tend to be more ambitious than other earth signs and are generally skilled at getting things done even when it seems impossible or unlikely. They enjoy doing things their way and are very independent individuals.

Effects

As the Sun enters Aquarius, those born under this sign will become more introverted and emotionally sensitive while becoming more intelligent, insightful, and analytical. They may also experience bouts of aloofness caused by their natural ability to focus all of their energy on whatever task they are trying to accomplish.

The Sun in this sign can cause one to become dreamy and detached from the rest of the world. These people will often have interests that are considered unusual by others. However, other people's views do not interest them as they're too focused on their projects or goals. These people are also likely to be very committed when it comes to the tasks they set out to accomplish, which can cause them to lose perspective on everything else that's going on around them.

Pisces: The Fish

In Pisces, also belonging to Jupiter, the Sun represents self-sacrifice, altruism, and a deep appreciation for spiritual matters. When traveling through this sign, the Sun can cause humans to have a strong need to put others' needs before their own. When the Sun enters Pisces on February 18, those born under these signs will find themselves drawn to humanitarian endeavors and a need to help others. They will also feel a strong need for spiritual fulfillment and possibly psychic awareness.

Element

The Pisces' element is water, which represents love and emotions. In Vedic astrology, the planet that rules over this sign is Jupiter (the son of Saturn). Water represents intelligence and imagination. Pisces is ruled by Jupiter, the planet that represents expansion. In Western astrology, Jupiter symbolizes good fortune and abundance. Because the water element is expanded by earth and its ruler (Jupiter), Pisces also signifies success.

People born under this sign can be very understanding, caring, loving, intelligent, artistic, and/or musical, depending on other astrological influences in their birth chart. Pisces natives are compassionate with a deep sense of spirituality, which others may or may not understand.

Symbol

According to Greek mythology, the fish was revered as it was considered a symbol of fertility, creation, and life. It was also believed to have been an "unbreakable" animal, explaining its ties to the earth with the world of the waters. The Pisces sign can symbolize a fluid connection between earthly desires and our spiritual self, or it may indicate that one is superior in understanding and communicating their emotions. The fish is a symbol of fertility, and in the zodiac, water flows around the Earth. Jupiter rules Pisces as well as Sagittarius.

Pisces represents our connection between the physical world and the spiritual realm. They may possess psychic or mystical abilities or feel drawn to topics of spiritual or psychic matters. Jupiter also rules Pisces, representing knowledge, expansion, luck, and abundance, indicating that a person with this sign will have an overwhelming sense of compassion for others. They may also be intelligent and full of imagination.

Characteristics

People with this sign will have varied interests, and they feel happy doing several different things. They typically enjoy being around others and love to make new friends. They also like having the freedom to do whatever they choose as far as their life choices. When the Sun is traveling through Pisces, people are likely to want to help others and be more caring than usual. They may engage in humanitarian endeavors and pursue spiritual fulfillment, or they might have heightened psychic awareness. Pisces natives are likely to experience a strong need for emotional intelligence in their choices and life plans.

People born under the sign of Pisces will often have a deep sense of spirituality. Although this sign is ruled by Jupiter, representing good luck and abundance, Pisces can also indicate strong psychic abilities. They may also be very compassionate, and understanding or they could develop these traits with time. This sign also symbolizes a fluid connection between the earthly desire for material gain and the spiritual self.

Effects

When the Sun is in Sagittarius, it represents our desire to expand and grow to better understand the world around us. When the Sun travels through Pisces, people are likely to feel a strong need for spiritual fulfillment or experience psychic awareness. They want to help others and may become more compassionate than usual. However, this sign is ruled by Jupiter, which helps Pisces people develop their imagination and love for exploration. They are often highly intelligent and creative.

In this chapter, you discovered the characteristics of four zodiac signs: Sagittarius, Capricorn, Aquarius, and Pisces. You also learned about these four placements' effects on a native being born under each sign. We also mentioned how the placement of the Sun in any given zodiac sign could affect people who were born under it. Now, you should better understand how these four signs differ, as two of them belong to Jupiter, the minister and advisor of the Sun, and the other two belong to Saturn, the son of the Sun, who is considered its biggest enemy. You learned what one could discover about themselves as the Sun moves from Sagittarius into both signs of Saturn, namely Capricorn and Aquarius, and finally finishes its journey in Jupiter's sign, Pisces. This transition affects a native and what it means in actual life.

Chapter 9: The Sun in Yoga

According to Vedic practitioners, yoga and astrology go hand in hand. Despite being different in terms of practice and actions, both focus on internal cleansing and spiritual healing. In a way, astrology and yoga form a symbiotic relationship. They share many principles like positive energy, chakras, and internal makeup. If applied correctly, both disciplines can become useful tools to combat adversities and feel at peace. Yoga and astrology have thrived for centuries, thanks to the work of many scholars, practitioners, and enthusiasts boasting the merits of each practice. They have successfully stood the test of time and are still used for spiritual cleansing today.

The Sun's Role in Yoga

Among all celestial bodies, the Sun, in particular, is closely associated with yoga and astrology. Yoga can help unravel the true potential and energy of the Sun, which can then be redirected towards internal healing. The Sun helps a person heal and feel alive, which is also one of the main goals of yoga. On cold winter days, the Sun's radiance and warmth feel comforting and uplifting. Similarly, yoga also helps us be at ease and rejuvenates our minds. When we connect with our inner selves, we feel just as warm and connected. In a way, both the Sun and yoga ignite the internal fire and illuminate our lives.

Several ancient Hindu accounts like the Yajurveda, Rigveda, and the Upanishads emphasize the importance of "Agni," the internal fire represented by the Sun. According to Ayurveda, Vedic astrology, and yoga, the Sun embodies sustenance and intelligence. Learning the right way to exude these qualities can truly change one's life, which is where yoga steps in. With consistent practice and deep learning, one can regulate their circadian rhythm and get more attuned to the Sun's vibrations and rhythms.

The Importance of Surya Namaskar

Surya Namaskar, or "Sun Salutation," is the act of worshipping or paying respect to the Sun by performing a set of asanas (postures). Surya translates to "Sun," and Namaskar translates to "salute." This practice is a form of modern Ashtanga yoga and should not be confused with Patanjali's Yoga Sutras. When performing a round of Surya Namaskar, the practitioner honors the Sun and thanks it for providing life and vitality. According to Vedic astrologers, this practice is the best way to honor the giant star's existence and its role in this universe. One round of Surya Namaskar comprises 12 asanas that are divided into two sets (one set comprises six poses, and the other set repeats the same poses in reverse order).

Each of these poses is meant to be performed specifically while maintaining composure and regulating your breathing pattern. Surya Namaskar has multiple benefits. Performing it regularly can help develop your physical strength and flexibility. It also helps release stress and keeps you calm. Astrologers suggest performing Surya Namaskar every day to strengthen the Sun's position in your horoscope and intensify its placement in your natal chart. With this, you can combat the ill effects of a weak or an afflicted Sun and reap more positive outcomes in your life.

Many practitioners have been performing Surya Namaskar for decades and swear by the positive benefits they have reaped. From weight loss to spiritual awakening, the benefits of Surya Namaskar are plentiful. Even though it takes time to notice positive results, the effects are life-changing and can replenish every form of your being.

The Twelve Steps and the Twelve Zodiac Signs

The twelve steps of Surya Namaskar reflect the twelve zodiac signs or constellations in the sky. Since the Sun follows a dedicated path to cross the sky over a year, it sits with every zodiac sign at some point. We can draw parallels between the chart of the zodiac constellations, and the twelve yoga poses to understand the manifestation of energy in all twelve pairings, one at a time. Let's take a look at each of these twelve Surya Namaskar poses and the right way to perform them, along with their connection to a specific zodiac sign.

Step 1: Pranamasana - Prayer Pose

Stand straight on your mat and bring your feet together. Keep your shoulders relaxed and expand your neck and chest. Take a deep breath, join your palms together, and place them in front of your chest. Exhale and hold this position for a few seconds.

Relation with Zodiac Sign: Aquarius

Planet: Saturn

Mantra: Om Mitraaya Namaha (One who is affectionate).

Step 2: Hastauttanasana - Raised Arms Pose

Take a deep breath and raise your arms above your head such that they almost touch your ears. Stretch your entire body from your feet to your fingers and feel the stretch in your spinal cord. Do not bend backward. Instead, keep your pelvis stretched towards the front.

Relation with Zodiac Sign: Pisces

Planet: Jupiter

Mantra: Om Ravaye Namaha (One who shines).

Step 3: Hasta Padasana - Hand to Foot Pose

Exhale and slowly bend your upper body from the waist until your nose almost touches your knees. Keep your spine straight, exhale, and stretch your arms toward the ground. Keep them straight and beside your feet. Try to touch the floor with your palms. You can slightly bend your knees at this point.

Relation with Zodiac Sign: Aries

Planet: Mars

Mantra: Om Suryaya Namaha (One who generates activity and disperses darkness).

Step 4: Ashwa Sanchalanasana - Equestrian Pose

Inhale and bring your left leg forward while pushing your right leg behind. Stretch it toward the back as much as you can. Place your right knee on the floor and let your palms touch the floor as you did in the previous step. The left foot should be straight and in alignment with both your hands. Look up and stretch your neck. Keep your spine straight.

Relation with Zodiac Sign: Taurus

Planet: Venus

Mantra: Om Bhaanave Namaha (One who shines).

Step 5: Dandasana - Stick Pose

Inhale and slowly push your left leg back while keeping your right leg stretched. With this, your body should form a straight line. Keep your arms straight and your palms touching the floor. Look down.

Relation with Zodiac Sign: Gemini

Planet: Mercury

Mantra: Om Khagaya Namaha (One who moves across the sky).

Step 6: Ashtanga Namaskara - Salute with Eight Points

Slowly straighten your hips to bring your entire body to the floor. Keep your palms on the floor and let your knees touch the floor as well. Once the body is aligned with the ground, raise your hips while keeping your knees on the floor. Slide your body to the front and let your chin and chest touch the floor. Your posterior should be slightly raised. With this pose, you are paying your respects to the Sun with eight points (two feet, two hands, chin, chest, and two knees).

Relation with Zodiac Sign: Cancer

Planet: Moon

Mantra: Om Pooshne Namaha (One who fulfills and provides nourishment).

Step 7: Bhujangasana - Cobra Pose

Straighten your knees and let your hips rest on the floor. Keep your palms on the floor and raise your upper back. Slide to the front and raise your chest. Bend your elbows and push your shoulders at the back. Inhale, look up, and bring your chest to the front. Exhale and push your tummy toward the floor. Tuck your toes and stretch your body as much as you can.

Relation with Zodiac Sign: Leo

Planet: Sun

Mantra: Om Hiranya Garbhaya Namaha (One who is filled with wisdom).

Step 8: Parvatasana - Mountain Pose

Exhale and slowly raise your hip area towards the ceiling while keeping your palms on the floor. Place your head between your arms and look down. Keep your knees and legs straight, and your heels should touch the floor. As you raise your tailbone and hips, your body should make an inverted "V" posture resembling a mountain.

Relation with Zodiac Sign: Virgo

Planet: Mercury

Mantra: Om Mareechaye Namaha (One who gives light).

Step 9: Ashwa Sanchalanasana - Equestrian Pose

Inhale and slowly release your hips to bring them back to the floor. Straighten your legs and let them rest on the floor. Bring your right leg to the front while pushing your left leg behind. Bend your right knee and place your right leg between your hands with your palms touching the floor. Your left knee and toes at the back should touch the floor. Try to push your hips down as much as you can. Look up and stretch your neck. Keep your spine straight.

Relation with Zodiac Sign: Libra

Planet: Venus

Mantra: Om Aadityaaya Namaha (The Divine Mother of the Cosmos, Son of Aditi).

Step 10: Hasta Padasana - Hand to Foot Pose

(This is the same pose you performed in step 3. It is important to perform a correct transition from the last asana to the next pose for effective results.) Raise your hips towards the ceiling and bend your upper body. Bring your feet together. Try to touch your knees with your nose while keeping your legs straight. Keep your arms straight and beside your feet. Try to touch the floor with your palms. You can slightly bend your knees at this point.

Relation with Zodiac Sign: Scorpio

Planet: Mars

Mantra: Om Savitre Namaha (One who takes responsibility for everything).

Step 11: Hastauttanasana - Raised Arms Pose

Slowly roll out your spine to raise your upper body. Inhale and raise your arms as you straighten your back and upper body. Your body should be perpendicular to the ground. Push your hips out and bend backward to stretch your body as much as possible. Your arms should be beside your ears. Stretch your entire body from your feet to your fingers and feel the stretch in your spinal cord.

Relation with Zodiac Sign: Sagittarius

Planet: Jupiter

Mantra: Om Arkaaya Namaha (One who is glorified and praised).

Step 12: Tadasana - Standing Mountain Pose

With this step, you are back to the initial position. Take a deep breath, join your palms together, and place them in front of your chest in a namaste position. Exhale and hold this position for a few seconds. Bring your arms down and loosen your body. Feel the sensations throughout your spine, arms, and legs.

Relation with Zodiac Sign: Capricorn

Planet: Saturn

Mantra: Om Bhaskaraya Namaha (One who spreads cosmic illumination and wisdom).

Spiritual practitioners advise doing Surya Namaskar early in the morning. With practice and consistency, you can increase one round per session. Practice it on an empty stomach to reap maximum health benefits as well. Over time, it will become a habit and a part of your routine.

The poses or asanas governed and shared by two zodiac signs at once are ruled by one planet. For example, poses 1 and 12 are related to Aquarius and Capricorn, respectively. Saturn rules both these signs. Since both poses are also the same, correspondence makes sense. The two asanas that occur just once in one round of Surya Namaskar (poses 6 and 7) are represented by the Moon and the Sun, respectively. Both the celestial bodies are independent and opposites, just like the two poses.

The Sun and Pranayama

The Sun is connected to Pranayama, which means "Purification of Breath." This breathing technique is quite popular among yogis and spiritual practitioners. Surya Bhedana is a Pranayama technique dedicated to the Sun. Surya means "Sun," and "Bhedana" translates to "piercing." This breathing technique is dedicated to the Sun and the Moon and their unison. The left nostril depicts the Moon and its calm energy, whereas the right nostril represents the Sun's activity, action, and heat. Surya Bhedana and Chandra Bhedana are related to the syllables "ha" and "tha," respectively. Collectively, they make the world "hatha," meaning "balance."

Basically, Pranayama is performed by blocking one nostril and letting air in through the other in an alternate manner, regulating your breathing pattern and restoring balance in your body. Surya Bhedana Pranayama enhances your "prana," or body heat, to induce vital force and improve your health. It also helps stimulate your mind and enhance your creativity. By learning the right form and practicing it consistently, you can put your plan into action and reach your goals with ease. Since the right nostril represents this Pranayama, you must breathe in through the right nostril and exhale from the left nostril to energize the Sun factors.

How to Perform Surya Bhedana Pranayama

Follow these steps to learn Pranayama the right way and reap its maximum benefit.

1. Pick a quiet spot and sit on a mat in a comfortable position. Keep your spine straight.

2. If you are seated in a cross-legged position, place the back of your left hand on your left knee, and join the tips of your thumb and index to make a circle.

3. Close your eyes and raise your right hand toward your face. Allow your middle and index finger to touch your forehead.

4. Use your ring finger to close your left nostril and breathe in through your right nostril. Hold your breath and place your thumb on your right nostril to block it. Lift your ring finger and allow the air to escape through your left nostril.

5. Repeat this in an alternate fashion by switching your finger and thumb to block each nostril in every round. Practice this for a few minutes.

This practice is related to the simple Pranayama breathing technique that uses the alternate breathing method. To perform Surya Bhedana Pranayama, breathe in through your right nostril and keep exhaling from the left without switching fingers.

Chakras Related to the Sun

The Sun is related to both the Solar Plexus chakra and the Crown chakra. In a literal sense, chakras translate to "spinning wheels" in Sanskrit. They are the energy centers within a body and are spread across the centerline of the body. Among the seven chakras that govern different body parts, the Solar Plexus (Manipura) and Crown (Sahasrara) chakras are closely associated with the Sun due to their matching frequencies. If you stand under the sunlight for a few minutes, both these chakras will receive energy and get cleansed. In a way, the Sun's energy balances these chakras, which are vital to improving your wellbeing and health.

Solar Plexus Chakra

The third chakra, also known as the "Manipura" chakra, is located at the center of the diaphragm. It governs your body's energy and symbolizes your identity and ego. It represents authenticity, personal freedom, willpower, and motivation. Due to its connection to the digestive system, this chakra is associated with the gut's brain and internal emotions. The color yellow represents this chakra. Like the Sun represents fire and heat, the Solar Plexus chakra is also represented by fire, which is also the chakra's main element. It uses heat and fire to regulate metabolism and maintain physical health.

How to Open the Solar Plexus Chakra

Opening your Solar Plexus chakra and balancing it is important. If left in an inactive state, you may suffer from intestinal or pancreatic problems along with emotional issues. To open or unblock this chakra, you must chant positive affirmations regularly. Practice visualization techniques to attract positivity and fend off negative energies. Another effective way is to perform yoga poses like Ardha Matsyendrasana (Half Spinal Twist), Dhanurasana (Bow Pose), and Paschimottanasana (Classical Forward Bend), which focus on improving your gut health and eliminating toxins from your body. Take a walk under the Sun and absorb morning sun rays for internal cleansing.

Crown Chakra

The Crown chakra is located above the head and acts as the center of wisdom, consciousness, enlightenment, and spiritual energy. An open Crown chakra can align with the universe's frequency and help you gain immense knowledge and creativity. It also establishes a deeper understanding of your surroundings and helps you tap into your spiritual energy. Both the Sun and the Crown chakras are related to masculine energy and divinity. Both are located at higher positions and act as governors. The Crown chakra reminds us that we are a part of the greater good and the universal forces instead of being alive as separate entities. We are an integral part of the cosmos.

How to Open the Crown Chakra

A blocked or closed Crown chakra can induce feelings of dissociation, boredom, general disinterest, and isolation. The person may feel stuck in a routine and detached from their life's purpose. In some cases, they may develop signs of depression or skepticism. To open your Crown chakra, engage in practices like visualization, journaling, and meditation. Certain yoga poses like Sasangasana (Rabbit Stand), Gomukhasana (Cow Face Pose), Ardha Ustrasana (Half Camel Pose), and Sirsasana (Headstand) can also help. More importantly, practice gratitude. Write down three things you are grateful for every day and feel blessed for being alive.

The Sun's Influence in Healing the Soul and the Mind

The Sun's energy and powerful rays can impact your physical health and make you stronger. Absorbing a healthy amount of sun can indeed help strengthen your internal system and rejuvenate certain parts of your body. For example, walking under the sun helps your body to get its daily dose of vitamin D, which regulates cell growth and reduces inflammation. It can also strengthen your bones. While the Sun provides various physical health benefits, it can also heal your mind and soul. People with little to zero sun exposure likely develop mental health issues like depression and moodiness over a prolonged period.

Sun rays also boost serotonin production, which can help you sleep better and improve your bedtime routine. You need quality sleep to function properly and keep your body and mind healthy. Sungazing is a practice followed for centuries and has been revered by ancient scholars for its benefits. This meditation practice allows your body to soak in the Sun's energy and feel recharged. Sungazing is known to be a booster for your soul and spiritual awakening. It promotes relaxation and inner peace, which are required to keep your soul happy.

Chapter 10: Keeping Your Soul Sunny

The Sun is life-giving, a blazing light in the midst of darkness. The Sun is the root of all life, and without it, we would be plunged into darkness. It is thanks to the Sun that you exist; it is the reason you are alive, breathing in the fresh air. The Sun is the reason everyone and everything you love exists.

Every single thing you come across on this earth is filled with energy. Everything embodies the energy of the Sun - the food you eat, the trees you see, and the people in front of you. Every aspect of this earth is alive and organic, brimming with the energy of the star of light. You may have noticed that the moon affects your mood on certain lunar days, such as the full or new moon day. In other words, you will often find that the changes in the moon affect your emotional state. Our minds, bodies, and hearts are all governed by external influence from the universe around us. The surrounding universe affects us because we are an entire universe ourselves. Each of us holds a whole universe within us – the energies of worlds, suns, moons, and stars exist inside us.

Humans are at their prime when they lead their life in tune with the Sun. Our circadian rhythm regulates our sleeping pattern, allowing us to shut down at nighttime and settle in for a restful sleep. Ayurvedic practitioners believe that metabolism is connected to the movement of the Sun, and that's why they advocate lunch as the biggest meal of the day, as the Sun is at its brightest during this time. You may feel tired and sluggish when you eat a lot at night, supposedly because the metabolism is slower when the Sun goes down.

Many engage in sunbathing as a way to receive physical health and spiritual benefits from the Sun. It is believed that this helps regulate the circadian rhythm, produce vitamin D, boost the immune system, and stimulate the pineal gland.

Light after Darkness

In life, we all go through moments of peril and darkness. Moments where it feels like we will never come out from under this blanket of darkness. Whoever we are and whatever we do, it is unlikely we will have escaped this blanket completely. It shows up in our lives seem to haunt or taunt us, to push us down a gloomy hole, one which we can barely scrape ourselves out of.

We live in a world of polarity, where there is darkness but also light. This darkness pushes us to go within, and that signifies it's time for a change. The darkness takes us for fools, but it has come to take us out of suffering.

In the physical world, every day, we witness the rising of the Sun piercing through the darkness of the night. It brings with it a glow, new hope, a fresh new start. The Sun says, come and try again; the doors of hope have arrived. Come and start fresh; the day is yours. This experience occurs within us, too. The light comes to disrupt the darkness, and we find that we must leap on this glimmer of hope! Just as the Sun rises every single day, so shall we. As we choose to mirror life's natural circles, we find ourselves moving back and forth between light and dark.

In those dark moments, we find ourselves cursing our bad luck, wishing we were someone else. But it is these moments that are vital to our growth. It is this darkness that is necessary for us to move fully into the light. It is this cyclical part of life that we must embrace. The sooner we begin to embrace the light, fully, deeply, the sooner we can come out of the darkness.

How to Embrace the Power of the Sun

The power of the Sun can aid your growth and guide your path towards spiritual evolution. Consider the magnitude of this life force. Perhaps in our modern, fast-paced lifestyles, we have become desensitized to just how incredible this star is. But you being here, reading this is your inner-self nudging you back to these primordial life forces. In ancient times, our ancestors understood nature. They understood how potent nature was, and they used it to heal and aid themselves. We, too, can use it in this way, despite all the commotion and rush surrounding us.

It's all about choosing to slow down and listen to our inner calling. *If your inner voice tells you to embrace nature as you have never before, now is the time.* Living in alignment with the Sun will help you become the healthiest and happiest version of yourself. Give it a go!

- Become an early-riser. In yogic traditions, the hours of the morning are said to have a certain spiritual power. This is the ideal time to meditate or practice yoga. 4-6 am is a potent time, helping to increase your mental clarity and positive energy. If you can't fathom waking up this early, try waking up 10-15 minutes earlier every day. This will help you slowly adjust to a different sleeping routine, and you will eventually notice the positive effects of being an early riser. It will help motivate you to continue on this Sun-seeking path.

- In Ayurveda, the Sun is considered the "source of all life." Another step to maintain a connection with the Sun is to honor it. Cultivating a practice of reverence is almost an act of rebellion in an age accustomed to social media likes and external validation. Self-esteem and personalities have been built around these online societies. Turning to the Sun and honoring it brings you back to your true self. Sitting in the Sun in honest gratitude opens your heart, mind, and soul back to the source of all things. You let this light enter and flow through you, healing you physically, emotionally, and spiritually.

- Sit in the Sun every morning, meditating or doing breathwork. Even a few deep breaths will help you build up this practice of presence and reverence. The idea isn't to worship the Sun but rather to allow the light of the Sun to remind us of the light within ourselves.

Each of us has a natural "sunlight" inside us. This light is our guide, our hope, and a source of healing. Connecting with the Sun gives us the power to remember this. This light can easily be snuffed out by the digital age, where we are racing against time to be the best in the eyes of others. It is a rarity to see someone slow down, feel grounded, and choose to reject these new societal norms.

The sunlight gives us this power. Its potency reminds us just how stunning, incredible, and life-giving we are. Each of us represents our own universe with our own Sun. This Sun within us is in our control, and we get to choose when it rises and when it sets. Choose every day to connect with the inner and external Sun. Choose to be light, choose to be sunny.

Healer

The Vedas worship this star of light. They view it as the source of light for the whole world. The light is not considered a material force but rather a power of love, life, and intelligence. The Sun is also not seen as an entity far away from us, but rather that its presence is here on Earth, touching our hearts and filling us with life.

The Sun is not simply seen as a physical star, for it represents the concept of light and consciousness. The Sun is merely a way to showcase these ideas. When deeply understood, the Sun is an internal source of energy. It is a doorway to a higher realm, a realm which we can travel through by harnessing the power of the Sun.

Worshipping the Sun is seen as a path to enlightenment and self-actualization. The Vedics observe a Sun ritual that involves making offerings to fire, connecting them with the powers of the Sun deity. They believe that we are all children of the Sun, existing on this Earth to bring the truth forward. For this reason, the Sun is considered to be at the core of who we are, with every soul being its own spiritual Sun.

The Gayatri mantra is one of the most important Vedic mantras and is often used in yogic practices. It is used to draw in the spiritual essence of the Sun, welcoming it into our mind, body, and heart.

We meditate upon the supreme light of the Divine transforming Sun (Savitri) that he may stimulate our intelligence.

The chanting of this mantra occurs at important points during the day, including sunrise, noon, and sunset. The power behind this does not simply represent the transformational power of the Sun but also the power of the spirits to take us out of the ego's darkness into the infinity of the authentic self.

Many parts of the world and religious texts revere the Sun and honor it, whereas, from a western perspective, the Sun is often feared. It is viewed as cancer-causing and skin-destroying. We are advised to cover up and slather on sunscreen at the smallest hint of sunray. Many believe that the Sun accelerates the aging process and ruins our health by causing skin cancer. Why is it that so many people around the world sunbathe, even worship the Sun, and do not find this to be the case?

We can use the intelligence held within the sunlight as a source of intellect, wisdom, and love. That said, how can we merge this with our current understanding of the Sun as being detrimental to our health?

There is plenty of literature on the health benefits of sunlight exposure which make for a greater understanding of how the Sun can benefit us in various ways.

One of the reasons the Sun is viewed as the meaning of life is because it is life-giving. Without it, neither we, nor animals, nor plants would breathe, eat, or grow. In light of this, returning to the Sun as a form of healing can grant us many great benefits. Experiencing this warm, healing light for a few moments in silence is a treasure in this age.

Positive Energy

Do you find yourself struggling to fight your inner demons?

Do you often experience moments of darkness?

Is there a part of you that wants to break free and unshackle itself?

The Sun is your answer, both physically and metaphorically. Begin a daily practice of honoring and spending time by yourself in the Sun. How this looks to you may not be exactly the same as other people practice, but you must make it your own. You may enjoy exposing your bare skin to the sunlight, reading a novel, doing yoga, or simply gazing up toward the Sun for a few minutes. Of course, you should practice safe sun exposure and not spend hours in direct sunlight. Moderate yourself and maintain a good balance so you can reap its physical and spiritual benefits.

The Sun's ability to detox further connects you with yourself, deepening your intuition and cultivating presence. Sunlight can be a potent cure against depression, grief, and misery. Many have found that a dedicated sunbathing practice has helped to cure many a depressive or dark episode.

Viewing yourself as being connected with the Sun will even allow your soul and personality to become sunnier and happier. Have you noticed how your mood changes on a sunny day compared to when it's gloomy? Truly, the Sun does fill you with positive energy! Even on the darker days, though, how do we keep this sunny energy within us? The sunlight inside us cannot always rely on the Sun itself; instead, we must cultivate a way to always be sunny without the Sun's warm and reassuring shine.

Here are a few ways you can implement this sunny mood into your everyday life:

- Practice gratitude. If this is difficult for you, concentrate on everything you are grateful to the Sun for. You'll soon realize the list is longer than you'd expect. From the fresh air you breathe to the food you eat, the Sun should be shown gratitude for these life-giving powers. As time goes on, it will become easier for you to find things about yourself and your life for which you are thankful. This practice begins to rewire your brain for positive thinking and self-fulfillment.

- Prioritize movement. How well does it feel being out in the Sun? That little sweat you break often feels like a detox. To keep your attitude and mood sunny, try and get some exercise every day, which is important for your emotional, physical, and mental health. We store so much stress, emotion, and pain in our bodies that working out can be a phenomenal relief. If you find it hard to go to the gym, begin by stretching at home, go on a jog, or play a follow-along exercise video suitable to your level.

- Cultivate presence. We have mentioned presence several times throughout this chapter, yet it is important to mention it again. Many of the problems we face mentally and emotionally often stem from overthinking. They arise as our minds constantly go in circles, thinking our way into problems. It is difficult for us to stop for a second and ground down into the here and now. How much of our environment do we truly notice and appreciate? Are we really here at all? The more present you can be, the more you realize how nonsensical many of your supposed problems are. The more present you are, the more space you have for joy, bliss, and happiness.

If you find it difficult to practice presence, which can be hard, especially with so many distractions, pointless screen time, and our busy lifestyles, here are some useful tips:

- Take a few moments during the day when you feel your feet on the ground, your legs on the chair, your back against the wall, or anything else that feels relevant in that moment. Notice these body parts – how they press down, how they're grounded. Embrace the sensations without thinking too much.

- Begin a meditative practice. A few minutes each day is a great place to start if you don't have a routine already, as the resistance levels may be high. Start small and slow, then witness your mind and practice grow before you.

- Stop and smell the flowers. Make it a point to start reconnecting with nature. The flowers on your morning commute, the trees that shed and grow leaves, the grass that you tread on every day. Start noticing these small things, and you will soon find it much easier to stay in the present moment.

The Sun has been a symbol of the self, the soul, and life since time immemorial. Sun worshipping has been around for thousands of years, with ancient civilizations devoting a true appreciation and understanding of this life-giving source. The Sun teaches us a valuable lesson, namely that life is for living. That every day we must rise and start anew. That new beginnings are for everyone.

The Sun is the clarity amidst confusion and distractions. In this world of fast-paced, active lifestyles, we face much fogginess. The Sun is the disruptor of not only the fog but the darkness, too.

Finally, the Sun we know teaches us much about our internal Sun. It is by having reverence and appreciation for the external Sun that our internal Sun begins to awaken. Connecting with this Sun helps to give us the motivation and inspiration to move forward in life, to feel true joy, bliss, and presence.

Conclusion

Congratulations for making it this far! Before you began exploring the different versions and roles of the Sun in astrology, as a timekeeper and a healing entity, you might have imagined this celestial body as nothing more than a ball of fire vital to the Earth's existence. As you flipped the pages, you realized that the Sun plays an even bigger role in the astronomical, medical, spiritual, and astrological domains. Now that you've gained insights into the Sun's role as a giver of life and have learned its significance in astrology, you are ready to harness its energy to revitalize your mind.

Let's recap all the insights we've gathered so far. The Sun plays an important role as a **life-giver** and in governing the planets within the solar system. The center of attention and the ruler of the planets, the Sun, has been the main deity in many belief systems that include solar motifs. The Sun God was the main ruler and influencer of the ancient Egyptians, Sumerians, and Indo-European people. Devotees sacrificed their lives and celebrated the Sun God's presence by observing rituals and offering prayers. According to them, pleasing the deity was indispensable as it procured healthy crops and governed the livelihood of all mortal creatures.

The Sun as a timekeeper has been a major subject of interest among scholars, intellectuals, and astrology enthusiasts. They studied the pattern of the Sun's location and movements to tell the time and determine the hours, days, weeks, months, and years. Ancient Greeks and Romans used devices such as sundials and water clocks designed based on the Sun's motion in the sky. The shadows on a sundial's surface formed a set of lines and angles that indicated a particular hour of the day. Water clocks were designed using a set of vessels with markings on the surface that helped the observer calculate the hour.

In Vedic astrology, the Sun is considered one of the most significant celestial bodies alongside the Moon. When a person was born, Vedic astrologers calculated the Sun's position to produce a natal chart, which represented the person's fate, personality, wealth, ambition, power, recognition, health, and fulfillment. The Sun stays in an exalted position when it meets Aries, thereby creating strong conjunction. By contrast, the Sun's debilitated position with Libra can negatively impact the native's life.

The Sun's **conjunction with other planets** is another interesting topic we've tapped into. An afflicted Sun in a horoscope can make the native's life worse. They are not given enough credit for their work and will likely suffer in their personal lives too.

The celestial body has also been a part of **Vedic and medical astrology** for many centuries now. Because it represents the heart, the Sun can help diagnose cardiovascular issues, making treatment easier.

It also represents a person's characteristics and determines their fate based on their sun sign. Lastly, the Sun's energy can be manifested by incorporating it into yoga practices and performing relevant asanas or breathing exercises. Surya Namaskar and Pranayama are two effective practices to harness the Sun's energy and heal your mental and spiritual health. When done correctly, they can also help open the Solar Plexus chakra and Crown chakra to improve your health.

Whether you are simply curious about exploring this new domain or wish to dig deeper in the study of the Sun in astrology, you can go back and refer to the relevant chapters and gain a better insight. If you think this book has helped you in any way, don't hesitate to spread the word and let your loved ones manifest the Sun's positive energy, too. Ask them to grab their copy and learn more about this ruling celestial body and its significance in astrology. Good luck, and happy manifesting!

Here's another book by Mari Silva that you might like

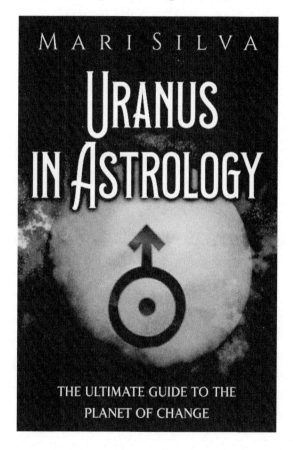

Your Free Gift (only available for a limited time)

Thanks for getting this book! If you want to learn more about various spirituality topics, then join Mari Silva's community and get a free guided meditation MP3 for awakening your third eye. This guided meditation mp3 is designed to open and strengthen ones third eye so you can experience a higher state of consciousness. Simply visit the link below the image to get started.

https://spiritualityspot.com/meditation

References

Planets – Sun. (2017, September 25). Retrieved from Horoscope website: https://www.astrology.com/planets/sun

The Sun in Astrology. (n.d.). Retrieved from Astrograph.com website: https://www.astrograph.com/learning-astrology/sun.php

The Sun in Astrology, the zodiac. (2015, May 8). Retrieved from Cafeastrology.com website: https://cafeastrology.com/sun.html

Ancient solar: How ancient civilizations harnessed the Sun's energy. (n.d.). Retrieved from Cleanchoiceenergy.com website: https://cleanchoiceenergy.com/news/Ancient_Solar

Cartwright, M. (2016). Surya. World History Encyclopedia. Retrieved from https://www.worldhistory.org/Surya/

Mishra, B. K. (2019, October 31). Sun God worshipped across cultures'. Retrieved from Times Of India website: https://timesofindia.indiatimes.com/city/patna/sun-god-worshipped-across-cultures/articleshow/71826105.cms

Team Vidhya Mitra. (2021, March 29). What is Sun in Astrology? What does Sun Represent in Vedic Astrology? Retrieved from Vidhyamitra.com website: https://vidhyamitra.com/sun-in-astrology/

Ancient Egyptian calendar: 1st calendar known to mankind. (2019, September 11). Retrieved from Egypttoday.com website: https://www.egypttoday.com/Article/4/74680/Ancient-Egyptian-calendar-1st-calendar-known-to-mankind

Early Roman Calendar. (n.d.). Retrieved from Webexhibits.org website: http://www.webexhibits.org/calendars/calendar-roman.html

Grattan, K. (2016, May 16). A brief history of telling time. The Conversation. Retrieved from http://theconversation.com/a-brief-history-of-telling-time-55408

Greek calendar. (n.d.). Retrieved from Worldtempus.com website: http://en.worldtempus.com/lexique/greek-calendar-108.html

Rajendran, A. (n.d.). What is Tithi in Hindu Calendar? – How is Thithi Calculated in Panchangam? Retrieved from Hindu-blog.com website: https://www.hindu-blog.com/2010/01/what-is-tithi-in-hindu-calendar-how-is.html

Short Guide on Nakshatras/Stars in Astrology - GaneshaSpeaks. (2017, February 20). Retrieved from Ganeshaspeaks.com website: https://www.ganeshaspeaks.com/astrology/nakshatras-constellations/

Telling the time with the Sun. (n.d.). Retrieved from Org.uk website: https://www.sciencemuseum.org.uk/objects-and-stories/telling-time-sun

The five building blocks of Panchang. (n.d.). Retrieved from Astrosage.com website: http://astrology.astrosage.com/2013/11/the-five-building-blocks-of-panchang.html

astrologerbydefault. (2019, June 24). psychologically astrology. Retrieved from Psychologicallyastrology.com website: https://psychologicallyastrology.com/2019/06/24/sun-mahadasha/

Effects of Sun in different houses. (2019, June 17). Retrieved from Astrotalk.com website: https://astrotalk.com/astrology-blog/effects-of-sun-in-different-houses/

Ghosh, A. P. K. (2020, December 16). Presence of Sun in 12 different houses of horoscope. Retrieved from Bigumbrella.co.in website: https://www.bigumbrella.co.in/presence-of-sun-in-12-different-houses-of-horoscope/

indastro. (n.d.). Sun planet – Sun effects in Astrology – Sun planet Astrology. Retrieved from Indastro.com website: https://www.indastro.com/planets/sun-planet.html

Sun & Moon Combinations: How Well do your Sun & Moon get Along? (n.d.). Retrieved from Southfloridaastrologer.com website: https://www.southfloridaastrologer.com/sun--moon-combinations-how-well-do-your-sun--moon-get-along.html

The connection between the Sun and moon in astrology. (2019, March 13). Retrieved from Askastrology.com website: https://askastrology.com/sun-and-moon-in-astrology/

Auspicious yogas formed by Sun in Vedic Astrology. (2019, December 18). Retrieved from Astrotalk.com website: https://astrotalk.com/astrology-blog/sun-in-vedic-astrology/

Conjunction Aspect meaning in astrology. (2018, January 29). Retrieved from Labyrinthos.co website: https://labyrinthos.co/blogs/astrology-horoscope-zodiac-signs/conjunction-aspect-meaning

Hall, M. (n.d.). Aspects to natal Sun in birth chart. Retrieved from Liveabout.com website: https://www.liveabout.com/sun-aspects-sun-signs-206275

Kahn, N. (2019, January 26). What conjunction, Trine, square, opposition, and sextile mean in astrology & birth charts. Retrieved from Bustle.com website: https://www.bustle.com/life/what-conjunction-trine-square-opposition-sextile-mean-in-astrology-birth-charts-13108526

Rosen, B. (2018, January 7). UNDERSTANDING PLANETARY COMBUSTION AND PLANETS TOO CLOSE TO THE SUN PART 1 - applied Vedic astrology. Retrieved from Appliedvedicastrology.com website: https://www.appliedvedicastrology.com/2018/01/07/understanding-planetary-combustion-planets-close-sun-part-1/

(Soni & View my complete profile, n.d.)

Soni, S., & View my complete profile. (n.d.). Vedic Astrology Research Portal. Retrieved from Blogspot.com website: https://astrologywithsourabh.blogspot.com/2015/05/all-about-planetary-combustion-in-vedic_62.html

Diseases in medical astrology. (2013, October 26). Retrieved from Astrovastutips.com website: https://astrovastutips.com/diseases-in-medical-astrology/

Kaushik, A. (2020, September 1). Nine planets & their associated herbs ! Ayurveda remedies. Retrieved from Astrokaushik.com website: https://astrokaushik.com/nine-planets-their-associated-herbs-ayurveda-remedies/

Medical Astrology - the planet and its related disease. (n.d.). Retrieved from Astrobix.com website: https://astrobix.com/learn/312-medical-astrology-the-planet-and-its-related-disease.html

Medical astrology and astrological medicine. (n.d.). Retrieved from Homeoint.org website: http://www.homeoint.org/morrell/astrology/medical.htm

Signs and remedies of weak Sun in horoscope - Ruby.Org.In. (2017, December 23). Retrieved from Org.in website: https://ruby.org.in/blog/signs-remedies-weak-sun-horoscope/

Vedic Medical Astrology - Medical Astrology - vedicnakshatras.Com. (n.d.). Retrieved from Vedicnakshatras.com website: http://www.vedicnakshatras.com/vedic-medical-astrology.html

View all posts by Dr. Deepak Sharma →. (2015, February 3). Heart attack and Astrology. Retrieved from Astroyantra.com website: https://www.astroyantra.com/heart-attack-astrology/

12 Astrology Signs. (n.d.). Retrieved from Astrology-prophets.com website: https://www.astrology-prophets.com/12-astrology-signs.php

12 Signs & their Significations (Part I). (2015, March 25). Retrieved from Theartofvedicastrology.com website: http://www.theartofvedicastrology.com/?page_id=127

Regan, S. (2020, May 30). Don't relate to your sun sign? It may be different in Vedic astrology. Retrieved from Mindbodygreen.com website: https://www.mindbodygreen.com/articles/how-to-calculate-your-sun-sign-in-vedic-astrology

Zodiac Constellations. (n.d.). Retrieved from Constellation-guide.com website: https://www.constellation-guide.com/constellation-map/zodiac-constellations/

12 Signs & their Significations (Part I). (2015, March 25). Retrieved from Theartofvedicastrology.com website: http://www.theartofvedicastrology.com/?page_id=127

12 Zodiac signs of Vedic Astrology. (2019, August 3). Retrieved from Astroved.com website: https://www.astroved.com/blogs/12-zodiac-signs-vedic-astrology

Dr R Nageswara Rao, vedic indian astrologer from http://www. askastrologer.com. (n.d.). Zodiac or rasi chakra in astrology and meanings of 12 zodiac signs in indian hindu vedic astrology. Retrieved from Askastrologer.com website: https://askastrologer.com/indian-hindu-vedic-astrology-zodiac.html

Hassan, A. D. (2015). Zodiac signs: The banished hero. Outskirts Press.

KellyWriter, A., & 12/07/, Z. (2020, December 7). What is Vedic astrology & how to find your Sun sign. Retrieved from Yourtango.com website: https://www.yourtango.com/2019327900/what-vedic-astrology-horoscope-meaning-each-zodiac-sign

Lesson 1. (2009, October 22). Retrieved from Astrojyoti.com website: https://www.astrojyoti.com/lesson1.htm

Astrologer, D. A. S. K. (n.d.). Zodiac Signs & lord Planets, Rashi Lords Astrology. Retrieved from Astrologer-astrology.com website: https://astrologer-astrology.com/zodiac_lord_indian_vedic_astrology_jyotish.htm

Rashi signs- free Indian astrology, 12 sun sign by name, Hindu zodiac signs. (n.d.). Retrieved from Astrodevam.com website: https://www.astrodevam.com/knowledge-bank/zodiac-sign-rashi.html?

Vallée, G. (2020, March 1). What's your Vedic astrological sign? Retrieved from Birla.ca website: https://birla.ca/en/whats-your-vedic-astrological-sign/

Zodiac signs: Significance of 12 sun signs. (2016, November 25). Retrieved from Ganeshaspeaks.com website: https://www.ganeshaspeaks.com/zodiac-signs/

(N.d.). Retrieved from Vedicfeed.com website: https://vedicfeed.com/traits-of-different-horoscopes-of-hindu-astrology/

Correlation between sun salutation and Vedic astrology. (n.d.-a). Retrieved from Altervista.org website: http://andreasyoga.altervista.org/sun-salutation-astrological-correlation/?doing_wp_cron=1629928290.3482990264892578125000

Correlation between sun salutation and Vedic astrology. (n.d.-b). Retrieved from Altervista.org website: http://andreasyoga.altervista.org/sun-salutation-astrological-correlation/?doing_wp_cron=1629969632.3922810554504394531250

Mahabir, N. (2021, March 17). Surya namaskar: How to do this warming yoga practice to connect to the rhythm and energy of the Sun. CBC News. Retrieved from https://www.cbc.ca/life/wellness/surya-namaskar-how-to-do-this-warming-practice-to-connect-to-the-rhythm-and-energy-of-the-sun-1.5951832

Manipura Chakra: Healing powers of Solar Plexus Chakra. (2020, September 3). Retrieved from Arhantayoga.org website: https://www.arhantayoga.org/blog/manipura-chakra-healing-powers-of-the-solar-plexus-chakra/

Mathur, N. (2020, February 16). Surya Namaskar (Sun salutations) and astrology. Retrieved from Cosmicinsights.net website: https://blog.cosmicinsights.net/surya-namaskar-sun-salutations-and-astrology/

No title. (n.d.). Retrieved from Com.my website: https://astroulagam.com.my/lifestyle/surya-namaskar-decoded-136815

Stokes, V. (2021, July 1). Want to harness the healing power of the Sun? Some say Sun gazing meditation can help. Retrieved from Healthline.com website: https://www.healthline.com/health/mind-body/sun-gazing

thejoywithin. (2019, July 30). How to do Surya bhedana pranayama: Sun piercing breath. Retrieved from Thejoywithin.org website: https://thejoywithin.org/breath-exercises/surya-bhedana-pranayama-sun-piercing-breath

Christopher. (2021, January 16). Sun symbolism (7 meanings in culture & spirituality). Retrieved from Symbolismandmetaphor.com website: https://symbolismandmetaphor.com/sun-symbolism-meanings/

Kelmenson, K. (2017, June 6). The potent power of the Sun. Retrieved from Spiritualityhealth.com website: https://www.spiritualityhealth.com/blogs/the-present-moment/2017/06/06/kalia-kelmenson-potent-power-sun

Sun: The eye of the world - spiritual Import of Religious Festivals. (n.d.). Retrieved from Swami-krishnananda.org website: https://www.swami-krishnananda.org/fest/fest_02.html

The Sun in the puranas and the Vedas. (n.d.). Retrieved from Scribd.com website: https://www.scribd.com/document/85910368/THE-SUN-IN-THE-PURANAS-AND-THE-VEDAS